Graven BREAD

They spoke of the God of Israel
as though he were one of the gods of the other peoples of the earth,
a work of human hands.

--2 Chronicles 32:19

By this author:

Quite Contrary:
A Biblical Reconsideration of the Apparitions of Mary

Geese in their Hoods:
Selected Writings on Roman Catholicism by Charles Haddon Spurgeon
compiled & edited by Timothy F. Kauffman

Graven Bread:
The Papacy, the Apparitions of Mary, and the Worship of the Bread of the Altar

To order additional copies of *Graven Bread* or *Quite Contrary,* or *Geese in their Hoods*, use the order forms at the back of this book, or write to:

White Horse Publications
P.O. Box 2398
Huntsville, AL 35804-2398

or call White Horse Publications directly at

1-800-867-2398

A complete listing of current White Horse Publications titles is contained at the back of this book.

Graven Bread

The Papacy,
The Apparitions of Mary, and
The Worship of the Bread of the Altar

by Timothy F. Kauffman

White Horse Publications
Huntsville, Alabama, USA

Graven Bread: The Papacy, the Apparitions of Mary, and the Worship of the Bread of the Altar

Cover design by Kevin Xiques
Photography by Greg Ray

Cover: A typical Eucharistic Adoration room.

Library of Congress Catalog Card Number: 94-90770
ISBN 0-9637141-2-0

First Edition 0 9 8 7 6 5 4 3

Additional copies of *Graven Bread* may be obtained by using the order forms at the back of this book, or by writing to:

White Horse Publications
P.O. Box 2398
Huntsville, AL 35804-2398
1-800-867-2398

This is dedicated to Jesus Christ:
my Lord, my God, my Master, my Savior.

He rescued me.

Acknowledgments

There are a great many people whom God has led into my life in order to make this publication possible. They prayed for me, discipled me, instructed me, encouraged me, loved me, and often admonished and corrected me. But as I grew to know each one of them, I began to realize that there was something that they loved more than me, something beside which even our friendship paled in significance. And if I learned anything from them at all, it was this: that God's Word is exalted above all other things. Though I could write for pages about the patience they showed me as they watched me grow and the many lessons they taught me, it suffices to say that their love for the Word affected me the most. Their respect for God's Word caused me to realize how precious it truly is, and to His Word I owe an immeasurable debt of gratitude. Through it, He changed my life, and because of that I will be, quite literally, eternally grateful.

Preface

> The Blood of Christ shed for our sake, and those members in which He offers to His Father the wounds He received... are no other than the flesh and blood of the Virgin: since, as St. Augustine said, 'the flesh and the blood of Jesus is the flesh of Mary.'
>
> --*Pope Leo XIII*

MEDJUGORJE, Bosnia, is the center of what could be considered the most powerful movement in the Catholic Church today. It is believed by millions that Mary, the mother of Jesus, has been appearing to six peasant children there since 1981 and has been giving them messages and instructions for the whole world. In the last 13 years, these simple children have done their job well. Millions of pilgrims from all over the globe have traveled to Medjugorje to experience peace and to listen to what the six visionaries, now adults, have to say. Thousands of messages from the apparition--or vision--of Mary have been written down by the visionaries, and then published and distributed throughout the world. It really is quite a phenomenon. The simple war-torn village of Medjugorje in former Yugoslavia has become a veritable Mecca for Catholics, many of whom braved the raging Yugoslav civil war of the early 1990s to visit the little town. But Medjugorje is not alone. There are presently hundreds of Marian apparition sites in the world today and a great many of them are located in the United States of America. Maryland, Georgia, California, Colorado, Arizona, and Texas have all recently been visited by this vision which calls itself Mary. Similarly, places like the Philippines, Venezuela, Ecuador, Ireland, Portugal, France and Italy have all in the past experienced, or are presently experiencing, the Marian apparition phenomenon. And like Medjugorje, these locations also have experienced a tremendous influx of pilgrims who want to find out what the apparitions of Mary are teaching.

Among the many topics which the apparition of Mary addresses in Medjugorje and throughout the world, there are two themes that surface more frequently than any other: obedience to the Pope and the worship of the Eucharist, which is the bread and wine of the Communion Sacrament. As many people know, the Eucharist is held by Catholics to be the literal body and blood of Jesus. Likewise, it is widely known that the Pope is held by Catholics to be the visible head of the Christian Church. These are both characteristically Roman Catholic doctrines. In that light, the visions of Mary in Medjugorje (and indeed in hundreds of other places in the world) can be considered to be a truly Roman Catholic phenomenon. Virtue and morality are often taught by the apparitions, but the most frequent teaching is about Catholicism. And if the teachings of the visions of Mary in any location in the world were to be summarized, it would suffice to say that they wish to see more people express obedience to the Pope, more people devote themselves to Mary, and more people worship the Sacrament of Communion.

The six visionaries of Medjugorje are not unaided in their efforts to evangelize the world with the teachings of the apparitions. There are many groups that have formed to assist them. One of them, and probably the most successful yet, is located in Birmingham, Alabama. *Caritas of Birmingham* is an organization devoted above all else to spreading the teachings of the Medjugorje apparitions. When the staff of *Caritas* was lamenting the success of Protestant evangelical efforts, they expressed surprise that it should be that way. After all, Catholics have the Eucharist, the True Church under the infallible guidance of the Pope, and the apparitions of Mary:

> "Many Protestant denominations are light years ahead of Catholics in their evangelical outreaches... yet we have the Eucharist, we have the Church, we have Our Lady. Things should be the other way around."[1]

---

[1] *Caritas of Birmingham*, June-October 1992 edition, "Caritas' Whole Mission to Undergo Complete Change," pp. 13-22

In its race to evangelize the world, *Caritas of Birmingham* expressed something that summarizes the teachings of every apparition of Mary to date: that the Catholic Church enjoys unique blessings which have been withheld from other Christian denominations. What are these blessings? The assistance of Mary through the Marian visions, the True Church under the infallible guidance of the Pope, and the True Presence of Jesus Christ in the Eucharist. These three working together in unison should make the Church invincible.

Thus, the subtitle of *Graven Bread*: "The Papacy, the Apparitions of Mary, and the Worship of the Bread of the Altar." It not only summarizes the expressed intentions of the apparitions, but also brings to mind the historic tendency of the first two to encourage the practice of the latter. Throughout history, pope after pope has encouraged adoration of the bread of the Communion Sacrament and sincere devotion to Mary. Vision after vision of Mary has returned the favor, encouraging obedience to the pope and worship of the Communion bread. This book was not written to establish this profound link between the teachings of the pope and those of the apparitions of Mary, but rather to discuss the profound spiritual ramifications of it. That the visions of Mary and the Papacy have agreed historically on matters of doctrine is not new to Catholics, and certainly should not be surprising to Protestants. The implications of the doctrines on which they have agreed, however, may be a different story altogether. *Graven Bread* was written to address them.

Introduction

This is because of what the LORD did for me when I came out of Egypt.
--Exodus 13:8b

THE celebration of Communion in the Church today is an act of obedience to the command of Jesus Christ. His words at the Last Supper were neither conditional nor optional. "Do this in memory of me."[2] But the celebration of Communion dates back much further than 30 AD when Jesus broke bread with His apostles the night before He died. The communion bread of which we partake today, while grounded in the New Testament mandate of Jesus Christ, has its origins in the book of Exodus. Jesus, in obedience to His Father, was celebrating a ritual that predated His incarnation by 1500 years: the Passover. When Jesus celebrated the Last Supper, He told His apostles, "I have eagerly desired to eat this Passover with you before I suffer."[3] And when God instituted the Passover ritual, He did so with the same mandate that Jesus used when He celebrated the Passover with His apostles. He told Moses to 'do this in memory of Me.' He instructed him to celebrate the Passover ritual with unleavened bread as a remembrance of what He had accomplished by setting the Israelites free from the Egyptian bondage:

> "For seven days you shall eat unleavened bread, and the seventh day shall also be a festival to the LORD. Only unleavened bread may be eaten during the seven days... On

---

[2] Luke 22:19b

[3] Luke 22:15

> this day, you shall explain to your son, 'This is because of what the LORD did for me when I came out of Egypt.'"[4]

Likewise, the meal that Christians celebrate today is in remembrance of what Jesus accomplished by setting us free from the bondage of sin through His death and His resurrection. Just like the Passover, Communion is a reminder to us of a past event, an accomplished fact. A remembrance.

In many Protestant denominations, this is called Communion.

In the Catholic Church, it is called the Holy Eucharist.

For many Protestant Christians the word 'Eucharist' is a foreign term, but to define the Eucharist as the Catholic equivalent of the Protestant Communion does not do the Eucharist justice. It is in fact much more than that, and Protestants rarely know even the smallest significance of the terms, rituals and traditions that make the Eucharist what it is.

For example, to a Protestant the term 'Eucharistic Adoration' would likely suggest a sacred form of worshipping God through the observance of the Lord's Supper. 'Eucharistic Adoration' might suggest to a Protestant the same form of worship we express when we partake of the Communion bread. It is true that one way Protestants offer worship to God is by remembering Him in Communion and obeying His commands, but this does not fully encompass the true meaning of Eucharistic Adoration.

Likewise, the term 'Perpetual Eucharistic Adoration' might imply to a Protestant a certain continuity of worship of God through participation in the Supper that He ordained--worshipful obedience offered to Him in perpetuity, without interruption. It is true that the Christian Church worships God continually through participation in the breaking of bread "until he comes,"[5] but again, this does not fully encompass the true meaning of Perpetual Eucharistic Adoration. Yet even among some Catholics the meaning of the Eucharist and the associated practice of Eucharistic Adoration often remains hidden, and the vocabulary is occasionally as foreign to them as it is to Protestants.

When I was in the process of purchasing a new car a year ago, I had the opportunity to test drive a vehicle with a salesman who

---

[4] Exodus 13:6-8

[5] 1 Corinthians 11:26

happened to be Catholic. During our conversation about the performance characteristics of the car, we discussed the fate of the first passenger to die in what was considered to be a relatively new and relatively safe car design. This led to a discussion about religious topics and ultimately led me to ask him about Eucharistic Adoration. He had never heard of such a thing. When I pressed him on the issue, he exclaimed, "I have been a Catholic for 46 years! If there were such a thing as Eucharistic Adoration, don't you think I would have heard of it by now?" Indeed, some time during those 46 years he should have heard of it, because Eucharistic Adoration is a central part of the Catholic faith. But his ignorance was no doubt the exception.

In fact, a great many Catholics, and a disturbing number of Protestants, not only understand the concept of Eucharistic Adoration, but wholeheartedly agree with it and wholeheartedly participate in it. And many Christians would be shocked to find out what Eucharistic Adoration truly is. And they would be shocked to discover how long it has been going on. And they would be shocked to discover how dangerously ignorant the Christian Church is of the widespread practice of Eucharistic Adoration. For it is not just a method of worshipping God by participating in the Sacrament of Communion. Rather, it is the worship of the Sacrament itself.

Part 1: Adoro Te Devote

And when we burned incense to the queen of heaven and poured out libations to her, was it without our husbands' consent that we baked for her cakes in her image and poured out libations to her?

--Jeremiah 44:19

Adoration of the Wafer

Lord and God, devoutly you I now adore;
Hidden under symbols, bread and wine no more.
--Thomas Aquinas, *Adoro Te Devote*

WHEN Jesus instituted the rite of Communion, or the Eucharist, He used the solemn words in reference to the bread, "This is My body." When He passed the cup, He said clearly again, "This is My blood." Analyzing Jesus' words here and His meaning when He used them will not be the central purpose of this book. The Catholic reader can therefore be assured that *Graven Bread* was not written to make a mockery of Transubstantiation. I strongly disagree with the Roman Catholic belief which holds that Jesus meant the bread literally became His body and the wine literally became His blood. However, though I disagree with this doctrine, I will not challenge it here. It should therefore not be inferred by the reader in any way that I am writing to dispute it. I do, however, intend to look well beyond the surface of the Eucharistic Sacrament.

One might question the need for stating the obvious--that Roman Catholics believe that the bread and wine literally become the body and blood of Jesus--but a discussion of the Eucharist makes that necessary. For while it is commonly understood that the Catholic Church teaches, and faithful Catholics believe, that the bread and wine of Communion become the true Flesh and Blood of Jesus Christ, very little is known among Protestants about what else the bread and wine are purported to contain.

The official doctrine of the Catholic Church states that the bread and wine of communion, the Eucharist, become the Body, Blood, *and* the Soul and Divinity of Jesus Christ. Once the bread and wine of Communion have been blessed and broken, or consecrated, there no longer exist bread and wine--only the appearance of them. To believe the contrary is considered to be un-Christian. The Council of Trent, in its definitive statement of Roman Catholic doctrine, expressed it in this manner:

> "If anyone shall deny that in the sacrament of the most Holy Eucharist are contained truly, really and substantially the body and blood together with the soul and divinity of our Lord Jesus Christ, and consequently the whole Christ, but shall say that he is in it only as in a sign, or figure or force--*anathema sit*."[6]

Anathema sit. 'Let him be accursed.' This is the same curse that Paul, in Galatians 1:8, called down on anyone who dared to preach another gospel than the one he preached. It is no small thing. It is an anathematization, a *de facto* excommunication from the Catholic Church.* As the Council of Trent stated, "Moreover, if anyone shall presume to teach, preach or obstinately assert, or in public disputation defend the contrary, he shall be *ipso facto* excommunicated."[7] Believing in the True Presence of the Body, Blood, Soul and Divinity of Jesus Christ in the Sacrament of Communion is an article of *fides catholica*, or obligatory faith. One cannot truly call oneself Catholic and at the same time reject the doctrine of the True Physical Presence of the Body, Blood, Soul and Divinity of Jesus Christ in the Eucharist during the consecration of the Mass.

Because of the change that is believed to take place during the consecration, it is considered improper to refer to the Communion elements as mere bread and wine after the priest has blessed them. There is no bread and wine--only the Body, Blood, Soul and Divinity of Jesus Christ. This was demonstrated recently when Bishop William K. Weigand of Sacramento, California, issued a statement calling for more reverence toward Jesus in the Blessed Sacrament. He requested that Catholics

---

[6] The General Council of Trent, Session XIII (1551): DS 1651

* One could argue that while the Council of Trent anathematized a great many people, the 1994 *Catechism* does not. This argument cannot stand long, however, for the 1994 *Catechism* quotes authoritatively from the Council of Trent no fewer than 80 times.(See the 1994 *Catechism of the Catholic Church*, pp. 721-2)

[7] The General Council of Trent, Session XIII (1551): DS 1661

> "...show reverence by refraining from needless chatter in church, by making a slight bow when receiving Communion, by referring to the consecrated Species as the Body of Christ or the Blood of Christ--and not 'the bread and wine.'"[8]

His statement reflects true and proper Catholic teaching. His instructions stem from the doctrine that once the consecration has been said by the priest, there no longer exists any bread or wine but only the Body, Blood, Soul and Divinity of Jesus *under the appearance* of bread and wine. And though Jesus and Paul both gave us the license we need to refer to the Communion meal as bread and wine, (i.e., they both referred to it as bread after it was blessed),[*] the Catholic Church still prefers that the faithful refer to it as the body and the blood.

I emphasize this not to attempt to disprove the doctrine, but rather to demonstrate the great importance that is placed on the doctrine by the Catholic Church. And participants in the Catholic Sacrament of the Eucharist must necessarily acknowledge this when they receive Communion. For example, when I purchased a First Communion kit from a local Catholic church bookstore, the kit included a *First Communion Remembrance Card* which had the following prayer written on the back:

> "My Lord Jesus Christ, I firmly believe that I am about to receive, in Communion, Your Body, Your Blood, Your Soul and Your Divinity. I believe it because You have said it, and I am ready to give my life to maintain this truth."[9]

This was from a prayer card for small children. One would be hard pressed to assert that steadfast adherence to this doctrine is not required of adult Catholics as well. It surely is.

---

[8] *The Wanderer*, Volume 127, number 32, August 11, 1994, "Sacramento Bishop Offers Some Liturgical Reminders," page 1

[*] See, for example, John 13:18 and 1 Corinthians 11:26-28. Because of these clear references by Jesus and Paul, I will exercise this license throughout the rest of the book and refer to the Communion elements as bread and wine, just as Jesus and Paul did.

[9] Prayer Card, *Remembrance of First Holy Communion*, no. 0065, © Fratelli-Bonella printers. This card accompanied the New *First Mass Book*, (New York: Catholic Book Publishing Co., ©1970-88)

Believing that the consecrated bread and wine contain not only the Body and Blood of Christ, but His Soul and Divinity as well, leads to the unique practice of Eucharistic Adoration. For if the bread and wine literally become the Body, Blood, Soul and Divinity of Jesus Christ, then the elements of Communion can be worshipped as God. Likewise, the elements of the Sacrament, which by their appearance seem to be just bread and wine, are to be carried in procession and worshipped. To believe the contrary is considered un-Christian. The Council of Trent stated it like this:

> "There is, therefore, no room for doubt that all the faithful of Christ may, in accordance with a custom always received in the Catholic Church, give to this most holy sacrament in veneration the worship of *latria*, which is due to the true God."[10]

> "If anyone shall say that in the holy sacrament of the Eucharist Christ, the only begotten Son of God, is not to be adored with the worship of *latria*, also outwardly manifested, and is consequently neither to be venerated with a special festive solemnity nor to be solemnly borne about in procession according to the laudable and universal rite and custom of the Holy Church, or is not to be set publicly before the people to be adored and that the adorers thereof are idolaters--*anathema sit*."[11]

Anathema sit. 'Let him be accursed.' To declare that the elements of Communion are not to be worshipped or carried in procession for the purpose of worship and adoration is an offense worthy of excommunication from the Body of Christ. To claim that those who worship the Communion bread are idolaters is an offense worthy of being, to borrow Paul's word, "accursed."

In order to appreciate the profound implications of this doctrine, one must study the manner in which it is applied by those who subscribe to it. For example, when Mother Teresa stated in 1993 that "Mary is our Advocate who prays to Jesus for us. It is only through the Heart of Mary that we come to the Eucharistic Heart of Jesus,"[12] she was referring to the fact that

---

[10] The General Council of Trent, Session XIII (1551): DS 1643

[11] The General Council of Trent, Session XIII (1551): DS 1656

[12] *Signs of the Times*, Volume 5, Number 4, September/October/
continued on next page

Jesus' living and Sacred Heart is believed to be present in the bread of the Eucharist. Mary's mediatrical role notwithstanding, Mother Teresa's sentiments regarding Jesus' 'Eucharistic heart' being present and accessible to us in the form or appearance of the bread and wine are consistent with the teachings of the Catholic Church. When Mother Teresa approaches Jesus Christ to worship Him in the Eucharist, she relies on Mary's assistance in doing so. And indeed, this application of the doctrine conforms perfectly with the clear statements of the Council of Trent.

The bread of Communion, being the True Presence of the Body, Blood, Soul and Divinity of Jesus Christ, is therefore the actual presence of Jesus Christ in the world today. He is held to be *physically present* in all of the Catholic Churches of the world. Because of this, there is even some speculation among well-studied Catholics that when Christ returns, He will reign for one thousand years, not in His glorified bodily form, but in His Eucharistic form--that is, in the form of the Communion bread. Bud Macfarlane, Sr., a prominent Catholic speaker, states,

> "He (Satan) will be defeated and then we will have the period of peace, where Jesus Christ reigns in whatever form, Eucharistic form, His actual physical form, or He reigns in His mystical body, which is another interpretation..."[13]

The understanding that Jesus may well reign in Eucharistic form is in complete harmony with the teachings of the Council of Trent. It was not taught outright by the Council, but the articles of faith which were defined there paved the way for such assertions as that of Mr. Macfarlane. Likewise the Eucharist, whether in the present time or during the Millennial Reign of Christ, is worthy of the adoration, veneration and worship that is very justifiably ascribed to God alone. And in accordance with the clear teachings

---

November 1993. Published by Signs of the Times, Sterling, Virginia, Maureen Flynn, editor. "Marian News Update: Lay Group Seeks New Marian Dogma," pp. 6-7

[13] Macfarlane, Sr., Bud, M.I., of The Mary Foundation, in his speech entitled, "The Coming Tribulations," to a group of Mary Foundation friends and benefactors on August 7, 1993, Westlake, OH. Parentheses added for clarity

of the Council of Trent, the Eucharist to this day is still carried in procession for the purpose of worship.

To honor the Sacrament in this way, some predominantly Catholic European cities still sponsor annual festivals during which the Blessed Sacrament, the Eucharist, is carried through town in processions lasting four to five hours. These processions include regular stops for the faithful to offer worship and adoration to the bread. Another aspect of this emphasis is the concept of Perpetual Eucharistic Adoration--uninterrupted periods during which the host is placed on display for continual worship by the faithful. The longest period of Perpetual Adoration on record is that which began in the Cathedral of Lugo, Spain in the fourth century and did not end until well after the Crusades against Jerusalem had ended.[14]

But this is not a fringe remnant of a long-abandoned ritual. Eucharistic Adoration--whether manifested in the form of a brief genuflection before the tabernacle where the Eucharist is kept, or in the form of perpetual worship--is a common form of veneration today and is practiced by faithful Catholics all over the world. For example, a recent issue of *The Mir Response*, a magazine dedicated to the distribution of the messages of the apparitions of Mary, included an article about the *Youth 2000* Prayer Festival scheduled for December of 1993. The article described the experience of a woman who had attended an earlier *Youth 2000* weekend and explained that the upcoming retreat would contain "over 40 hours of opportunity to adore Jesus in the Eucharist." Her own *Youth 2000* weekend had begun with an explanation of the reverence that would be expected for Jesus in the Eucharist, the consecrated bread which would be on display in an adoration room throughout the three-day retreat. And though many of the youth had never before experienced Eucharistic Adoration, they accepted it at once and began to practice this new form of worship immediately:

> "There were no moans or groans, no complaints [from the youth], just open acceptance of what was required... They came to understand the 'why' for genuflecting in respect to

---

14 Cruz, Joan Carroll, *Eucharistic Miracles and Eucharistic Phenomena in the Lives of the Saints*, (Rockford, IL: Tan Books and Publishers, Inc., ©1987) pg. 284

> Jesus and without hesitation knelt on both knees each time they entered the room or crossed the room before Our Lord. Some even went a step further and kissed the ground before Jesus and some never turned their backs on Him as they would leave the room walking backward, always facing Jesus. Sound extreme? Not so! It was the most reverence that I have ever seen!"[15]

Her assessment of the practice of Eucharistic worship was quite accurate. The reverence which the youth expressed toward the Eucharist that weekend was a sound reflection of the doctrines of the Catholic Church. What the children did that weekend was not extreme in the least. Rather, it was an obedient response to what Pope John Paul II has been preaching since the beginning of his pontificate, and what the Papacy has been preaching for centuries.

In his 1980 letter of instruction *On Certain Norms Concerning the Worship of the Eucharistic Mystery*, John Paul II wrote, "The venerable practice of genuflecting before the blessed sacrament, whether enclosed in the tabernacle or publicly exposed, as a sign of adoration, is to be maintained. ...In order that the heart may bow before God in profound reverence, the genuflection must be neither hurried nor careless."[16] Then, in his 1993 address to the 45th Eucharistic Congress in Seville, Spain, he stated that his desire is to establish Perpetual Eucharistic Worship in every Christian community in the world:

> "I hope that this form of Perpetual Adoration, with permanent exposition of the Blessed Sacrament, will continue into the future. Specifically, I hope that the fruit of this Congress results in the establishment of Perpetual Eucharistic Adoration in all parishes and Christian Communities throughout the world."[17]

---

[15] *The Mir Response*, Volume 5, No. 4, August/September 1993 edition, pp. 8-9, 21. Published by the MIR Group, New Orleans, LA, 70151, Mimi Kelly, editor, "Falling in Love ...With Jesus." Brackets added

[16] Pope John Paul II, Instruction *Inæstimabile Donum,* Sacred Congregation for the Sacraments and Divine Worship: "On Certain Norms Concerning Worship of the Eucharistic Mystery," section B, Eucharistic Worship Outside Mass, article 26, February 24, 1980

[17] Pope John Paul II, June 1993, Seville, Spain. Address to the 45th

continued on next page

John Paul II's sentiments are in perfect conformity with those of his predecessor, Pope Leo XIII. In Leo XIII's 1902 Encyclical Letter *Miræ Caritatis*, he wrote,

> "It gives Us much pleasure to recall to mind that We have officially approved and enriched with canonical privileges not a few institutions and confraternities having for their object the perpetual adoration of the Sacred Host; that We have encouraged the holding of Eucharistic Congresses... For as a right faith teaches us to acknowledge and to worship Christ as the sovereign cause of our salvation... so the same faith likewise teaches us to acknowledge Him and to worship Him as really present in the Eucharist."[18]

There are many different terms for it, but they all mean the same thing: Adoration of the Wafer, Eucharistic Adoration, Worship of the Eucharist, Adoration of the Sacred Host, Adoration of the Blessed Sacrament, Worship of the Eucharistic Mystery, or Eucharistic Worship. All of these terms mean that what were once bread and wine literally become the Body, Blood, Soul and Divinity of Christ, and it is therefore proper to bow down to and worship it as if in the very presence of God. The teachings of the Catholic Church have encouraged this practice to this day, the popes have practically mandated it, and the faithful have obeyed for more than 1500 years. Worship of the Eucharist is a very common practice in the Catholic Church. I strongly disagree with the practice itself, and I strongly disagree with the claims of the True Presence and Divinity of Jesus in the Eucharist. However, let it suffice to say for now that it is indeed what the Catholic Church believes to be the truth. Because of the belief that the Eucharist contains the very divinity of Jesus Christ, the Catholic Church has erected the Eucharist as an object that is to be worshipped.

Eucharistic Congress. *Signs of the Times*, Volume 6, Number 2, April/May/June 1994 edition, "Perpetual Adoration of the Holy Eucharist," pp.10-11

[18] Pope Leo XIII, Encyclical Letter *Miræ Caritatis*, May 28, 1902

The Sacrifice of the Mass

And while they presume much on their own sacrificial victims, they do not realize that they are immolating them to deceitful and proud spirits...
--Augustine, *The Trinity*, Book 4, Chapter 14

THIS need not be a lengthy chapter. Jesus Christ, after stating at the Last Supper that the bread and wine were His body and blood, commanded us to partake of it in remembrance of Him. We were to celebrate Communion, or the Eucharist, in memory of what He did for us on the Cross. However, the Catholic teaching on Communion is that since the bread and wine become the Body, Blood, Soul and Divinity of Jesus Christ, then our celebration of Communion is not a mere remembrance of Calvary--it is rather a *participation* in the Sacrifice that was offered there. The Catholic communion service, informally called the Mass, is in reality called *the Sacrifice* of the Mass, and is purported to be a participation in the One Sacrifice that Jesus offered on the Cross. As such, the Mass is held to be effective as a propitiation, or payment, for sins. Indeed, the wafer of bread that is offered up in the Sacrifice of the Mass is called 'the Host,' from the Latin word, *hostia*, meaning 'victim of sacrifice.'[19] It is no great leap of logic to realize that if the Host is the True Body, Blood, Soul and Divinity of Jesus Christ, then Jesus Christ is the sacrificial victim of the Sacrifice of the Mass, and this is precisely what the Catholic Church teaches. The 1994 *Catechism of the Catholic Church*, citing the Council of Trent, states,

---

[19] Hardon, John A., S. J., *The Modern Catholic Dictionary*, (New York: Doubleday & Company, Inc., ©1966) pg. 258

> "The sacrifice of Christ and the sacrifice of the Eucharist are *one single sacrifice*.* 'The victim is one and the same.'"[20]

If Christ's Sacrifice on the Cross was *the* payment for the sin of the world, and the Sacrifice of the Mass is considered to be a participation in that payment, then the Sacrifice of the Mass is held to be as effective as the Crucifixion in removing iniquity. To believe the contrary is considered un-Christian. The Council of Trent, the definitive doctrinal council of the Catholic Church, stated it in this manner:

> "And inasmuch as in this divine sacrifice which is celebrated in the Mass there is contained and immolated in an unbloody manner the same Christ who once offered himself in a bloody manner on the altar of the cross, the Holy Council teaches that this is truly propitiatory and has this effect... For, appeased by this sacrifice, the Lord grants the grace and gift of penitence, and pardons even the gravest crimes and sins."[21]

> "If anyone shall say that in the Mass a true and real sacrifice is not offered to God, or that what is offered is nothing but that Christ is given us to eat--*anathema sit*."[22]

> "If anyone shall say that the sacrifice of the Mass is only one of praise and thanksgiving; or that it is a mere commemora-

---

* So highly esteemed and closely guarded is this doctrine of the perpetuated sacrifice of Christ that it is maintained, amazingly, by some faithful that the Eucharist will be the 'daily sacrifice' (Daniel 11:31) which is abolished by the anti-Christ. (See *The Thunder of Justice*, by Ted and Maureen Flynn, (Sterling, VA: MaxKol Communications, Inc., ©1993) pp. 249-51). The apparitions of Mary have frequently taught this interpretation to their followers. Interestingly, the fruit of this teaching is that those who worship the Eucharist do so more frequently, and with greater fervor, the more the doctrine of Eucharistic Worship is called into question.

20 *The Catechism of the Catholic Church*, Part 2, Section 2, Chapter 1, Article 3.V, "The Sacramental Sacrifice: Thanksgiving, Memorial, Presence," paragraph 1367. Copyright ©1994, United States Catholic Conference, Inc. Emphasis in original

21 The General Council of Trent, Session XXII (1562): DS 1743

22 The General Council of Trent, Session XXII (1562): DS 1751

> tion of the sacrifice consummated on the cross but not a propitiatory one--*anathema sit*."[23]

Anathema sit. 'Let him be accursed.' This anathema is assigned to anyone who does not believe that the celebration of Communion is effective in removing sin from the person who participates in it. The curse is for anyone who does not believe that the act of communion is in reality the sacrifice of Jesus Christ's Body, Blood, and His Soul and Divinity on the altar, offered to God as a reparation for sins.

The Order of the Mass, in accordance with the doctrines so-defined at Trent in the 1500s, naturally reflects the sacrifice that was being described at this Council. During the Sacrifice of the Mass, when the priest is about to administer Communion to the faithful, he first offers it to God, on His "altar in heaven," as a payment for sins:

> "We offer to you, God of glory and majesty, this holy and perfect sacrifice... Look with favor on these offerings and accept them... Almighty God, we pray that your angel may take this sacrifice to your altar in heaven. Then, as we receive from this altar the sacred body and blood of your Son, let us be filled with every grace and blessing."[24]

Jesus Christ is therefore believed to be offered to God on the altar in Heaven as a sacrifice for sins. It is through this sacrifice that the Catholic is to receive graces, blessings, and atonement for wrongdoings.

This is indeed what the Catholic Church teaches. In addition to worshipping the Eucharist, the Catholic is also taught that the bread and wine of the altar, the Blessed Sacrament, are offered as a sacrifice for sins. I strongly disagree with these doctrines, but I will not contend with them here. I only wish to familiarize the Protestant reader with what is practiced in the Catholic Church and to establish that the Catholic Church teaches that the elements of Communion are literally offered as a sacrifice in payment for sins.

---

[23] The General Council of Trent, Session XXII (1562): DS 1753

[24] *Sunday Missal Prayerbook and Hymnal for 1994*, "Eucharistic Prayer Number 1," (NY: Catholic Book Publishing Company, ©1993) pg. 27

The Testimony of Two

> On the testimony of two or three witnesses a fact shall be established.
>
> --2 *Corinthians 13:1*

THERE is a phenomenon in the world today--a phenomenon with which Protestants are all too unfamiliar and which many Catholics hold dear to their hearts--and its presence in the world contributes significantly to the propagation of Eucharistic Worship. This phenomenon is known by several different names but it is most commonly referred to as an 'apparition of Mary,' or a 'vision of Mary.' It is purported that Jesus' mother, Mary, is currently appearing in many different locations with a message for mankind, an urgent plea to return to the one true faith of Rome. These visions are presently occurring in so many cities in the world that it would be an inefficient use of space to name them all. However, to gain some indication of the pervasive presence of the apparitions of Mary in the world today, consider just a few of the places they are currently visiting:

Conyers, Georgia, USA
Lubbock, Texas, USA
Emmitsburg, Maryland, USA
San Francisco, California, USA
Kibeho, Rwanda, Africa
El Cajas, Ecuador
Finca, Betania, Venezuela
Denver, Colorado, USA
Agoo, La Union, Philippines
Medjugorje, Bosnia
Phoenix, Arizona, USA
San Nicolás, Argentina

The list really could go on and on, as there are presently (at the very least) 30 apparition sites active in the United States alone.[25] But let it suffice to say that reports of Marian visions are

---

[25] *The Washington Post*, Volume 117, number 313, October 14, 1994,

continued on next page

currently very frequent and widespread. And though it can be said that the apparition phenomenon is presently at its most extensive level ever, it can also be said quite accurately that the past 1200 years have not been exempted from these visions either. For centuries, the apparition of Mary has visited many of the Catholic faithful, and has done so in cities all over the world. To gain some indication of the pervasive presence of the apparitions of Mary in the past, consider just a few of the places they have visited in just the last five hundred years:

Rue de Bac, Paris, France (1830)	Garabandal, Spain (1961-1964)
Akita, Japan (1973-1981)	Lourdes, France (1854)
Fátima, Portugal (1917)	Guadalupe, Mexico (1531)
Beaurang, Belgium (1932)	Zeitun, Egypt (1968-1970)
Knock, Ireland (1879)	Naju, South Korea (1973)
Pontmain, France (1871)	Agreda, Spain (1617)

These apparitions, both past and present, are often accompanied by apparitions of Jesus (e.g., at Conyers, Georgia, USA) or by apparitions of Michael the Archangel (e.g., at Garabandal, Spain). However, the central theme in all of them is Mary and her role in bringing God's message to mankind.

Neither of the two previous lists of past or present apparitions can be considered representative of the large number of purported apparitions in the world today or in history. There were in fact nearly 300 apparitions world wide from 1923 to 1975,[26] and there have been well over 300 visions of Mary since then.[27] And every place that the apparitions occur, they communicate messages to the few visionaries who actually see them. Their messages contain words of encouragement and perseverance, as well as instructions to adhere to the true faith, to stand firm in defense of Catholic doctrine and to distribute these respective messages as widely as possible. It would be difficult and even tedious to go

---

"For Thousands, the Virgin Mary Is a Vision of Hope," pp. A1,24

26 *Our Lady Queen of Peace*, "Apparitions of Mary Throughout the World," Special Edition I, 2nd Printing, Winter 1992, Dr. Thomas Petrisko, ed. Pittsburgh Center for Peace, McKees Rocks, PA, 15136, pg. 1. Used by permission

27 Macfarlane, Sr., Bud, M.I., "Marian Apparitions Explained," recorded on May 18, 1991 at St. Leo's Catholic Church, Elmwood, NJ

into every detail of every topic of the apparitions' teachings, but several common threads surface almost universally among the thousands of messages: the primacy of the Pope, the True Presence of the Body, Blood, Soul and Divinity of Jesus Christ in the Sacrifice of the Mass, and the Worship of the Eucharist.

This chapter was not written to refute any one of these doctrines, and neither was it written to prove or disprove the authenticity of any of the apparitions. Rather, I wish only to establish that the apparitions of Mary have emphasized these doctrines and that together, the popes and the apparitions have encouraged the practice of Eucharistic Worship. What follows is a catalog of messages from apparitions of Mary, (and occasional apparitions of Jesus or Michael) throughout the world and throughout history. They all reflect, to varying degrees, the instructions of the Papacy: that the Eucharist is a true and effective sacrifice for sins, that it contains the Body, Blood, Soul and Divinity of Jesus Christ, and that the faithful should bow down before the Sacrament of Communion and worship it.

Instructions from the apparitions of Mary on the True Physical Presence of Christ in the Bread, the Sacrifice of the Mass, and the Worship of the Eucharist:

Apparition of Mary to the children of Medjugorje, Bosnia 1981-present

> "It is very beautiful to remain Thursdays for the adoration of my Son in the Blessed Sacrament of the Altar."[28]
>
> "Unceasingly adore the Most Blessed Sacrament of the Altar."[29]
>
> "Continually adore the Most-holy Sacrament (the Eucharist). I am always present when the faithful are in adoration."[30]

---

[28] *Words From Heaven: Messages of Our Lady from Medjugorje*, 5th ed., (Birmingham, AL: Saint James Publishing Company, ©1991) pg. 269. Message of May 28, 1993. The authors wished to be known only as, "Two friends of Medjugorje."

[29] *Words From Heaven*, pg. 162. Message of March 15, 1984

[30] O'Carroll, Michael, CSSp, *Medjugorje: Facts, Documents, Theology,* *continued on next page*

Apparition of Mary to Sister Agnes Sasagawa, Akita, Japan 1973-1981

> "Do you say well the prayer of the Handmaids of the Eucharist? Then, let us pray it together: 'Most Sacred Heart of Jesus, truly present in Holy Eucharist, I consecrate my body and soul to be entirely one with Your Heart, being sacrificed at every instant on all the altars of the world..."[31]

Apparition of Mary to Gladys Quiroga de Motta, San Nicolás, Argentina 1983-1990

> "Jesus, the Eucharist! It is His living and true Body; adore It and love It. ...It is in the Eucharist that He becomes again Body and Blood."[32]

Apparition of Mary to Therese Lopez, Denver, Colorado, USA 1991-present

> "Our Lady came as the Blessed Sacrament was being placed on the altar... She said, 'I have come to pay homage to my Son.' ...she remained in adoration and ...said to me, 'Bring my children here. I like it here.' ...When Our Lady spoke of bringing her children here, she was referring to adoration of the Blessed Sacrament; for she is with each of us when we are in adoration of her Jesus."[33]

> "My Dear Child, the sacrifice of the Mass must be the center of your life. ...Every day, [God] sends His Son to the mystery

---

(Dublin, Ireland: Veritas Publications, ©1989) pg. 160. Message of March 15, 1984. Parentheses added for clarity

[31] *Our Lady Queen of Peace*, "Church Approves Messages, Weeping Statue as Supernatural," pg. 16. Message of July 6, 1973. Used by permission

[32] *Our Lady Queen of Peace*, "An Urgent Appeal: Our Lady in Argentina," pg. 7. Message of June 1, 1986. Used by permission

[33] Kuntz, J. Gary, *Our Holy Mother of Virtues: Messages for the Harvest*, Volume 1, (Denver, CO: Colorado MIR Center, ©1992) pp. 59-60. Message of October 24, 1991

of the cross, making Him to be ever present with him in the sacrament of the altar."[34]

Apparition of Michael the Archangel to Lucia Abóbora, Fátima, Portugal 1916

"Most Holy Trinity, Father, Son, Holy Spirit, I adore You profoundly and offer You the most precious Body, Blood, Soul and Divinity of Jesus Christ, present in all the tabernacles of the earth, in reparation for the outrages, sacrileges, and indifference with which He Himself is offended."[35]

Apparition of Mary to Maureen Hinko, Seven Hills, Ohio, USA 1985-present

"Our Lady came in gray and a gold color. She bowed before the Eucharist. She said, 'Give praise, honor and glory to Jesus, ever-present in this Holy Sacrament of the Altar.'"[36]

Interior Locution of Mary to Cyndi Cain, Bella Vista, Arkansas 1989-present

"The Holy Sacrifice of the Mass is the most complete, most perfect of all prayers. ...At the moment of Consecration all the Heavenly Hosts adore the True Presence upon bended knee. Their adoration continues even when the Sacred Host is reposed in the Tabernacle. ...The Holy Eucharist must be preserved. You must come and adore and reverence your God and King if you would persevere in the Time of Darkness."[37]

---

[34] Kuntz, pg. 58-9. Messages of September 29 and October 7, 1991. Brackets added for clarity. "He" was used in the original, but "God" was the intended meaning.

[35] Walsh, William Thomas, *Our Lady of Fátima*, (New York: Doubleday & Company, Inc., ©1947, 1954) pg. 41

[36] *Holy Love: Messages from Our Blessed Mother Leading Souls to Holiness*, (Seven Hills, OH: Our Lady's Foundation, ©1994) pg. 26. Message of September 3, 1993

[37] *A Call to Peace*, Volume 4, Number 5, "Locutions from the Hidden Flower of the Immaculate Heart," pg. 7. Message of April 25, 1993

"I urge again devotion to my Son in the Most Blessed Sacrament, and ask all to work for Adoration of Him in this Sacrament of Love... Do not believe any who scoff or ridicule such devotion, nor the Adoration of Jesus Christ in the Monstrance.*"[38]

Interior Locution of Mary to Don Stephano Gobbi, Italy 1973-present

"It is Jesus Who is present under the white appearance of the Eucharistic Bread. ...your prayer, your love and your life are directed to Jesus in the Eucharist. You are being called more and more to become apostles and new martyrs of Jesus, present in the Eucharist. And so you must increase your reparation, your adoration and your life of piety."[39]

"You are gathered in prayer with me--by the recitation of the Holy Rosary, with your listening to my word, with the Holy Hours of Eucharistic Adoration."[40]

Apparition of Mary to Sister Mary of Agreda, Spain *circa* 1617

"The Virgin Mother, in her retreat, prostrated herself on the ground and adored Her Son in the Blessed Sacrament with incomparable reverence. Then also the angels of her guard, all the angels of heaven, and among them likewise the souls of Enoch and Elias, in their own name and in the name of the holy Patriarchs and prophets of the old law, fell down in

---

* The Monstrance is, in practical terms, an ornate display case in which the Eucharist is exposed for public or private adoration. Though many are in the shape of a sunburst, the photographs on the front and back covers of *Graven Bread* depict a cross-shaped monstrance.

38 *A Call to Peace*, vol. 4, no. 2, "Locutions from the Hidden Flower of the Immaculate Heart," pg. 7. Message of January 9, 1993

39 *Signs of the Times*, volume 6, number 2, "Eucharistic Messages from Heaven," pp. 14-18, by Maureen Flynn. Message of June 13, 1989

40 *Our Lady Queen of Peace*, "Interior Locutions," pg. 6. Message of November 14, 1990. Used by permission

adoration of their Lord in the Holy Sacrament." (From the description of Mary's reverence during the first Mass)[41]

Apparition of Mary to Nancy Fowler, Conyers, Georgia, USA 1987-present

"We need to pay more attention to the Eucharistic Jesus, and go to the Mass. Both Our Lord and the Blessed Mother have said that there is no place where more graces are given than at Mass. The greatest place for healing is the Mass. Jesus is there, waiting for us to love Him, adore Him and thank Him."[42]

This is by no means an exhaustive list, but the display of support which the apparitions of Mary show for the papal doctrines is obvious. In addition to the emphasis placed on the Eucharistic doctrines, the apparitions of Mary have also shown outwardly their emphatic support for the doctrines of the primacy of the pope as the visible head of the Body of Christ. What follows is a catalog of messages from apparitions of Mary throughout the world and throughout history. They all reflect to varying degrees the support that the apparitions have demonstrated for the authority of the Papacy.

Messages from the Apparitions of Mary on the primacy of the Pope:

Apparition of Mary to the children of Medjugorje, Bosnia 1981-present

"Have him (the pope) consider himself the father of all mankind and not only of Christians."[43]

---

[41] Mary of Agreda, *Mystical City of God*, Volume IV, *The Coronation*, (Hammond, IN: W. B. Conkey Company, ©1914) pg. 565, para. 666

[42] *To Bear Witness that I Am the Living Son of God, Vol. 1: Reported Teachings and Messages to the World from Our Lord and Our Loving Mother*, (Newington, VA: Our Loving Mother's Children, ©1991) pg. 19

[43] *Words From Heaven*, pg. 105. Message of September 26, 1982. Parentheses added for clarity

Apparition of Mary to Gladys Quiroga de Motta, San Nicolás, Argentina
1983-1990

> "The priests must follow the pope for to walk by him is to walk by my Son Himself."[44]

Interior Locution of Mary to Don Stephano Gobbi, Italy
1973-present

> "This great apostasy is spreading more and more [unchecked]... When my Pope speaks with courage and reaffirms with force the truths of the Catholic faith, he is no longer listened to and is even publicly criticized and derided."[45]

Apparition of Mary to Juan Angel Collado, Sabana Grande, Puerto Rico
1953

> "By these times, the Holy Father (the Pope), a preferred and true son, will have visited the land (referring to a visit by the Pope)... It is necessary that the Holy Father appeal to all priests, religious, bishops and the chosen ones so that united with all the children of the church, the rosary be prayed imploring the conversion of all men."[46]

Interior Locution of Mary to Cyndi Cain, Bella Vista, Arkansas
1989-present

> "Be always humble, obedient children to my beloved Pope John Paul II. He truly is the Vicar of Christ, the visible Head

---

[44] *Our Lady Queen of Peace*, "An Urgent Appeal: Our Lady in Argentina," pg. 7. Message of October 27, 1986. Used by permission

[45] *Our Lady Queen of Peace*, "Interior Locutions," pg. 6. Message of June 11, 1988. Used by permission, brackets added for clarity

[46] *Our Lady Queen of Peace*, "Our Lady of the Rosary in Puerto Rico," pg. 13. Message of April, 1953. Used by permission. Parentheses added for clarity

of the Church on Earth. He is guided by the Holy Spirit. Do not listen to those who speak against him, nor the ones who act contrary to his teachings and authority."[47]

Interior Locution of Mary to Gianna Talone Sullivan, Emmitsburg, Maryland, USA 1992-present

"Little ones, I thank you for your prayers for your country and I ask you to continue to pray for your country and for My beloved pope."[48]

Apparition of Mary to Maureen Hinko, Seven Hills, Ohio, USA 1985-present

"And you must be careful to remain faithful to Church Tradition as it stands now under John Paul II."[49]

Again, these lists are by no means exhaustive. They are, however, representative of the sentiments that the apparitions of Mary in the past and in the present have expressed toward the Papacy, the doctrine of the True Presence of Jesus Christ in the bread and wine, the Sacrifice of the Eucharist, and the practice of Eucharistic Worship. This is not to dispute the primacy of the pope or the doctrine of the True Presence, but rather to establish that the apparitions are in agreement with, if not in submission to, the pope in regard to the teachings that the Papacy has propagated and the authority which it has wielded.

There are literally hundreds of thousands of apparition messages, both currently and throughout history, but the central theme of the apparitions of Mary has been to recognize the

---

[47] *A Call to Peace*, Volume 5, Number 9, "Locutions from the Hidden Flower of the Immaculate Heart," pg. 4. Message of July 28, 1994

[48] From the message network of "Our Lady's Message To The World Through Gianna Talone Sullivan" at St. Joseph's Church, Emmitsburg, MD. Message 36, August 4, 1994. These messages are from a relatively new apparition and are not yet in publication.

[49] *Holy Love: Messages from Our Blessed Mother Leading Souls to Holiness*, pg. 2. Message of March 21, 1993

authority of the Papacy by honoring the doctrine of transubstantiation and the practice of Eucharistic Worship. The followers of the apparitions have recognized this important relationship. In a special 'Eucharistic' edition of *Signs of the Times,* a magazine dedicated to the propagation of the messages of the apparitions of Mary, an article appeared under the title "Our Lady of the Most Blessed Sacrament." That article was divided into two sections titled "Mary And The Eucharist" and "Marian Shrines Are Eucharistic Shrines," respectively. The article stated,

> "The inseparable bond that exists between Mary and the Eucharist is brought out in several ways. ...But perhaps nowhere is the close link between the Mother and Son, Immaculate Virgin and Eucharistic Christ, more apparent than in the Marian shrines that are found throughout the world. ...Our Lady asked that a church be built on the site of Her apparitions at Lourdes, which of course indicates that She wanted the Eucharistic Sacrifice to be celebrated there."[50]

Likewise, the organization called *Caritas of Birmingham* has recognized this relationship as well. One of its outreach efforts involved a 30-second television commercial which encouraged devotion to the Eucharist and a return to the Catholic Church. The title of the commercial spot reveals *Caritas'* acknowledgment of the connection between the apparitions of Mary and the Eucharist. In fact, the Eucharist, which was originally purported by the Roman Church to be the Lamb of God in the form of bread, has now been called "The Lamb of *Mary*" by the staff of *Caritas*:

> "The Lamb of Mary is a ministry which produces TV commercials, camera-ready ads, brochures, flyers, and other media to inform the world about Our Lady's plans in Medjugorje. ...Its original plan was to produce one evangelistic commercial, some of which was filmed in Medjugorje, about the Eucharist. We had no idea that this 30 second spot, called 'The Lamb of Mary,' would evolve into a ministry."[51]

---

[50] *Signs of the Times*, Volume 6, Number 2, April/May/June 1994, "Our Lady of the Most Blessed Sacrament," pp. 25-27

[51] *What is Caritas of Birmingham?*, a tract explaining the mission of *Caritas of Birmingham,* 1991

This connection that has been acknowledged by *Caritas of Birmingham* and *Signs of the Times* magazine is consistent with every apparition on record, whether approved by the Church or not. The apparitions' followers have been very astute in recognizing this key correlation between the spiritual manifestations of the apparitions and the presumed manifestation of the True Presence of the Body, Blood, Soul and Divinity of Jesus in the Sacrifice of the Mass. The purpose of this chapter, therefore, is to demonstrate the public acknowledgment of the link both by the apparitions themselves, and by their many followers. The apparitions of Mary adamantly support the doctrines established by the Papacy and emphatically insist that its followers bow down before and worship the Eucharist. The connection is something that Catholics not only know about, but of which they are also quite fond.

The apparitions of Mary have indeed honored the authority of the Papacy and have instructed the faithful to put into practice what the popes have taught. It can be said, therefore, that if the Papacy has established the doctrines of transubstantiation and the True Physical Presence of Jesus in the Eucharist, then the apparitions of Mary have erected the Eucharist for worship in honor of the Papacy.

The Life of the Flesh

> Since the life of a living body is in its blood, I have made you put it on the altar, so that atonement may thereby be made for your own lives, because it is the blood, as the seat of life, that makes atonement.
>
> --*Leviticus 17:11*

WHILE retaining the appearance of bread and wine, the Sacrament of the Eucharist is purported to transcend physical reality and become true flesh and true blood. Because the bread and wine continue to appear as such after the blessing of the priest, the presence of the body and blood of Jesus must be taken on faith. Catholics therefore believe in the transformation in spite of what their senses may tell them. The bread of Communion continues to taste like bread, and the wine continues to taste like wine, but just as Jesus instructed us to believe without seeing, the Catholic Church has instructed its members to believe without tasting.

But such faith is necessary no longer. As if in response to the doubts of Protestants, and even of some Catholics, countless miracles involving the Eucharist have been observed--miracles which are understood to demonstrate the True Presence of the Body and Blood of Jesus--and all of them have been recorded in great detail by the clergy of the Catholic Church. Some of the miracles have been dismissed as legend, but most have received official approval of the Church, and all of them relate to adoration of the Sacrament of Communion. Some of the miracles involve a piece of consecrated bread, the host, surviving extreme circumstances unharmed, and others involve extraordinary events in the lives of the saints when they were in the presence of the Eucharist. Some have experienced rapture or ecstasy, often levitating several feet above the ground for hours on end, a phenomenon known to affect more than 200 saints of the Catholic Church, including such notables as Theresa of Avila and Alphonsus de Liguori.[52] Others have recorded very emotional religious experiences in which they felt a oneness with Christ, and indeed felt that they had been ushered into His very presence by receiving the Holy Eucharist. Catherine of Siena and Clement of Ancyra, among many others, were purported to have experienced this phenomenon, claiming that they had received communion personally from Jesus Christ Himself.[53] All of these miracles are presumed to be evidence of the doctrine of the True Presence, and serve as "…a strong reminder of the real presence of Jesus in the Eucharist."[54]

But one specific type of Eucharistic miracle is especially curious since it involves the flowing of blood from the communion bread. On many occasions consecrated bread has been known to bleed profusely, staining the cloth of the altar with fresh blood, and even giving the appearance of severed veins inside the bread as if an unseen heart was pumping blood through the wafer. Examples of this peculiar phenomenon are myriad, and many of them have been approved by the Magisterium of the Catholic Church.

One such miracle is that of the Bleeding Host of Santarem, a miracle that took place early in the 13th century. The miraculous host is still on display at the Church of the Holy Miracle in Santarem, Portugal, and has received validation even from members of the medical field:

> "The Host is somewhat irregularly shaped, with delicate veins running from top to bottom, where a quantity of blood is collected in the crystal. In the opinion of Dr. Arthur Hoagland, a New Jersey physician who has observed the miraculous Host many times over a period of years, the coagulated blood at the bottom of the crystal sometimes has the color of fresh blood, and at other times that of dried blood. This miracle… has endured for over 700 years."[55]

---

[52] Cruz, pp. 266-7
[53] Cruz, pg. 233, 238-9
[54] Cruz, pg. 48
[55] Cruz, pg. 39

Such also was the case in Alatri, Italy in 1228 when a young girl, wishing to use a consecrated host as an ingredient for a love potion, was surprised to see it turn into flesh and blood before her eyes. "To her horror she saw that the Host was no longer like bread, but had turned the color of flesh--which she knew to be alive." When the miracle was reported to Pope Gregory IX, he approved it, and thus began a sincere veneration which continues to this day. The miraculous host is placed on display for adoration and worship twice yearly, and in 1978, the 750th anniversary of the miracle, the wafer was carried in worshipful procession through the streets of Alatri.[56]

Another interesting miracle involving a bleeding wafer is that which occurred in Siena, Italy in the year 1330. Apparently, a priest had consecrated the wafer of bread and then treated it disrespectfully by placing it between the pages of his prayer book instead of in a pyx, the proper carrying case for a consecrated host. When he arrived at his destination, he opened his prayer book to find that the pages were now soaked red with the blood of the Eucharist. Only one page of the priest's prayer book survives to this day, but it has been approved as a relic worthy of veneration by such popes as Gregory XVI, Boniface IX, Gregory XII, Sixtus IV, Innocent XIII, Clement XII, and Pius VII.[57]

These miracles have proliferated throughout the history of the Catholic Church, but there is one common string that cannot go unmentioned here: the apparitions of Mary. These Eucharistic miracles are purported to testify to the Doctrine of the True Presence of Jesus in the bread and wine, but they are also believed to substantiate the claims of the apparitions. One of the most well-known Eucharistic miracles today is that which is currently taking place in Betania, Venezuela, which is also the location of one of the most prominent Marian apparitions of our time:

> "In addition to the profound spiritual conversion taking place [in Betania], incredible phenomena has(sic) deepened the faith of many. Phenomena of various sorts has(sic) been reported. ...It is believed, however, that of all the signs the most powerful and significant manifestation of God's love was given on December 8, 1991, on the feast of the Immaculate

---

[56] Cruz, pp. 30-7,300-1

[57] Cruz, pp. 86-8

> Conception. During the celebration of the Holy Mass, Fr. Otty Ossa Aristizabal, the main celebrant of the vigil Mass, had just consecrated the host when an incredible miracle occurred: 'I consecrated the host and I broke it into four parts. I ate one of the parts and left the other three parts of the host on the plate after I gave grace. When I looked into the plate I could not believe my eyes when I saw a red stain forming on the host, and from it a red substance was beginning to emanate, similar to the way in which blood spurts out from a puncture. After the consecration, I took the host and protected it in the sanctuary. The next day at six in the morning, I observed the host and I found that the blood was still fresh and that it had trickled down, and that is what has appeared on the photograph. After that I put the host in the Monstrance, ...so the faithful ones could observe it.'"[58]

Tom Rooney, who was at Mass that day, witnessed the miracle personally and even captured on video tape the flowing of blood from the consecrated host. He stated, "...I could see the blood flowing out of the host. It was just, it was just flowing down, and you could see it collecting in the bottom of the glass. It was the most incredible thing you could possibly imagine, ...and you could see that it was blood. There was no mistaking it."[59]

In order to verify that the red liquid flowing from the Eucharist and coagulating on the altar was truly blood, "the bleeding host was then taken to the bishop's residence and later submitted for thorough medical examinations at a leading forensic laboratory in Caracas, Venezuela, whose technical and scientific expertise is nationally recognized. The results of that investigation revealed a startling discovery: the substance excreted from the host was found to be human blood."[60]

Another such Eucharistic miracle is that which occurs regularly in Agoo, La Union, Philippines, the location of another continuing apparition of Mary. Judiel Nieva, the visionary in Agoo, has been experiencing and receiving messages from visions

---

[58] "Betania: Land of Grace," a video narrated by Ricardo Montalban. Directed, written and produced by Drew J. Mariani, Marian Communications, Ltd., ©1993

[59] "Betania: Land of Grace"

[60] "Betania: Land of Grace"

of Mary since 1989. But the central focus of his visions is the miracle which takes place when he receives the Eucharist:

> "Residents of Agoo, which has a population of about 42,000, claim Nieva is a seer and that Communion wafers and wine turn to flesh and blood in his mouth."[61]

Likewise, in Naju, South Korea, a woman named Julia Kim receives messages from visions of Mary. To prove that it is really from God, the vision of Mary has provided Julia with Eucharistic miracles which are supposed to authenticate her experiences:

> "On several occasions, the Sacred Host which Julia received has bled in her mouth. In May 1991, this Eucharistic miracle occurred in the parish church in Naju, where Julia and thirty-three pilgrims from the Philippines were attending Mass. When Julia began to taste blood in her mouth, she went to the chapel administrator. She opened her mouth, and the administrator saw the Host become a light brown color, then turn to a deep, blood red. The Host continued bleeding, and soon Julia's mouth was filled with Blood. Partly because of this miracle, many people, including [Jaime] Cardinal Sin, wholeheartedly accept Julia's extraordinary experiences as coming from God."[62]

These miracles in which the host begins to bleed or turns to flesh are surprisingly common events at or near Marian apparition sites. By far the most dramatic Eucharistic miracles, though, are those in which the Eucharist does more than bleed. It pulsates with the rhythm of a beating heart. One such miracle occurred in January of 1994, also in the Philippines:

> "In the adoration room of the Center for Peace, Asia, in the Philippines in January 1994, two college students participating in Eucharistic Adoration witnessed what they described as the 'throbbing or pulsation' of the Blessed Sacrament. The

---

[61] *The Tennesseean*, Volume 89, Number 66, March 7, 1993, "Filipinos flock to glimpse vision of Mary," pg. 2A

[62] *Signs of the Times*, Volume 6, Number 2, "Modern Day Miracles of the Eucharist," pp. 12-13. Brackets added

two young men, Nestor Ramon Tesoro III and Lailani DaSilva, were there as part of the weekly youth cenacle."[63]

The same phenomenon was experienced recently in Ogden, Utah, USA, where a parish priest noticed that the cup which held the wine during Mass began to feel sticky with a strange liquid. When he looked down he noticed red drops of blood on the altar. This has been happening repeatedly for Lawrence Sweeney, the priest at Holy Family Catholic Church, but the miracles did not stop with the bleeding chalice:

> "On January 6, 1994, the Feast of the Epiphany, a new phenomenon occurred. Those present at a Holy Hour talk given at the parish by Steubenville president Father Michael Scanlon, OFM, saw the Blessed Sacrament pulsating, in the same rhythm as a beating heart. Scores of parishioners witnessed the event. One doctor in attendance captured the beating Host on videotape."[64]

As strange as it may seem that the bread of communion begins to bleed or pulsate, these many miracles are being captured on video cameras and in photographs. And before such technology was available, the hierarchy of the Catholic Church was providing the necessary authentication. This phenomenon has been occurring for centuries and it has obviously been influenced by the presence of the apparitions of Mary. What is the purpose of these miracles? *Signs of the Times* magazine put it rather succinctly when it stated, "Part of the providence of these events was the *timing*. Not only did the Eucharistic occurrences begin on a special feast day, the Feast of Corpus Christi, but in addition, they also followed a Gallup poll which found the majority of Roman Catholics in the United States do not believe in the Real Presence of Christ in the Eucharist."[65]

Well-timed indeed. The miracles serve to honor the Papacy in its claims that the bread and wine become the Body, Blood, Soul and Divinity of Jesus Christ. The apparitions of Mary have

---

63 *Signs of the Times*, Volume 6, Number 2, pp. 12-13

64 *Signs of the Times*, Volume 6, Number 2, pp. 12-13

65 *Signs of the Times*, Volume 6, Number 2, pp. 12-13. Emphasis in original

demonstrated great consistency in that regard, and have honored the claims of the Papacy by supporting the doctrine of the True Physical Presence at every turn.

Many other such miracles as those described above have been recorded in detail by the Catholic Church and by the followers of the apparitions of Mary. But the matter at hand is not so much that the consecrated wafers bleed or pulsate, but of what the bleeding signifies. Leviticus 17:11 states that the life of the flesh is in the blood, so it is no great leap of reason to understand why these miracles of blood issuing from the bread are significant. They indicate that the Eucharist has been given a life of its own. Life has been given to the Eucharist by the apparitions of Mary, and so convincingly that many of the miracles of the Eucharist involve the bread actually becoming flesh and blood in the mouths of those who receive it, and pulsating while the faithful adore it. The Eucharist, which the apparitions of Mary have erected for worship in honor of the papacy, has been brought to life.

The Freedom of Speech

> They have hands but do not feel,
> feet but do not walk,
> and no sound rises from their throats.
> --*Psalm 115:7*

IN addition to the miracles which involve bleeding and pulsating hosts, and the diverse phenomena associated with them, many miracles have been recorded in which a consecrated wafer has actually spoken to the faithful who were in adoration. According to Joan Carroll Cruz, author of *Eucharistic Miracles*, "Many saints have had the privilege of hearing the voice of Jesus speaking from consecrated Hosts."[66] For example, when Clare of Assisi feared that the German heresy being led by Emperor Frederick II in the mid-1200s would adversely affect the nuns at the Convent of San Damiano, she bowed in desperation before the Eucharist, imploring God to protect her. At that moment, she heard the voice of Jesus saying out loud from the consecrated host, "I will have thee always in my care."[67]

Another example is that of Anna Maria Taiga, a 19th-century Blessed* of the Church. Once while she was in adoration of the Eucharist, she experienced a vision in which she saw a lily appear in the wafer. At the same time, she heard a voice saying, "I am the

---

[66] Cruz, pg. 249

[67] Cruz, pg. 249-50

* This is one of several steps involved when a person is declared a saint by the Catholic Church. The three main levels of progression are these: Venerable, Blessed, and Saint.

flower of the field, the lily of the valley. I am thine alone."[68] Likewise, when Paul of the Cross was about to participate in a crusade against the Turks in the 18th century, he heard a voice speaking from the tabernacle where the Eucharist was kept. The voice instructed him not to participate in the crusade, but rather to establish a new religious order in Jesus' honor.[69]

Blessed Alan de la Roche, a Dutch visionary through whom the apparition of Mary gave the Rosary to the Catholic Church in 1463, also experienced a similar encounter with a speaking host:

> "One day when he [Alan de la Roche] was saying Mass, Our Lord, Who wished to spur him on to preach the Holy Rosary, spoke to him in the Sacred Host: 'How can you crucify Me again so soon?' Jesus asked. 'What did You say, Lord?' asked Blessed Alan, horrified. 'You crucified Me once before by your sins,' answered Jesus, 'and I would willingly be crucified again rather than have My Father offended by the sins you used to commit. You are crucifying Me again now because you have all the learning and understanding you need to preach My Mother's Rosary, and you are not doing so. If you only did this you could teach many souls the right path and lead them away from sin--but you are not doing it and so you yourself are guilty of the sins they commit."[70]

Margaret Mary Alacoque, a 17th century visionary, was known for her apparitions of Jesus in the form of His Sacred Heart. She often received messages from that apparition and frequently spent time adoring the Eucharist. During Mass one day, Margaret Mary was about to receive Communion when she heard the voice of Jesus speaking from the consecrated wafer:

> "As I went up to receive Him in Holy Communion, He showed me His Sacred Heart as a burning furnace, and two other hearts were on the point of uniting themselves to It, and of being absorbed therein. At the same time He said to me: 'It is thus My pure love unites these three hearts forever.' He

---

68 Cruz, pg. 254

69 Cruz, pg. 249

70 de Montfort, Louis, *The Secret of the Rosary*, (NY: Montfort Publications, ©1965-92) pg. 23, trans. Mary Barbour, T.O.P. Brackets added for clarity

afterwards gave me to understand that this union was all for the glory of His Sacred Heart, the treasures of Which He wished me to reveal…"[71]

This occurrence of the voice of 'Jesus' speaking from the host in order to encourage further devotion was repeated in the case of Lucia Abóbora when she was concerned about a certain form of Marian devotion that she was being asked to support. In her concern, she knelt before the Eucharist in the Tabernacle in order to obtain further instruction from 'Jesus':

> "On December 17th, 1927, she went before [the Eucharist in] the tabernacle to ask Jesus how she should comply with what had been asked of her, that is, to say if the origin of the devotion to the Immaculate Heart of Mary was included in the Secret that the most holy Virgin had confided to her. Jesus made her hear very distinctly these words: 'My daughter, write what they ask of you. Write also all that the most holy Virgin revealed to you in the Apparition, in which she spoke of this devotion. As for the remainder of the Secret, continue to keep silence."[72]

A more recent example is that of Mother Angelica, hostess of the *Eternal Word Television Network* (*EWTN*) cable television show, "Mother Angelica: Live." Her devotion to, and adoration of, the Eucharist is widely known, and in many photographs she can be seen wearing a Eucharistic necklace prominently over her habit. The necklace is in the form of a Monstrance, the container in which the consecrated host is put on display for worship and adoration. When Mother Angelica was once asked about the financial and emotional hardships she endured when *EWTN* was just getting started, she explained that she heard Jesus speak to her while in adoration of the Eucharist:

---

[71] Lord, Bob & Penny, *This is My Body, This is My Blood: Miracles of the Eucharist, Book II*, (Westlake Village, CA: Journeys of Faith, ©1986) pg. 236

[72] Abóbora, Lucia, *Fatima In Lucia's Own Words: Sister Lucia's Memoirs*, Kondor, Louis, SVD, ed., (Still River, MA: The Ravengate Press, ©1976) pp. 189, 195. Lucia here writes her account in the third person. Brackets added for clarity

> "It seemed everyone was against us, the Church, bankers, lay people, everybody saying we can't do it; this is foolish! So, I went before the Blessed Sacrament; I was very angry, and I said, 'Lord, I told You, I'm not the one for the job. Why me?' And suddenly, as I felt this so deeply, I heard the Lord say very distinctly, 'Yes, and why Me?' I never asked again."[73]

A similar experience has been reported by the Conyers, Georgia visionary, Nancy Fowler. In the book in which the Conyers apparition's messages are published, it was reported that 'Jesus' speaks to Nancy in the Eucharist while she is in adoration and that she has in the past taken dictation directly from the voice that speaks to her there:

> "While Nancy was praying in front of the Blessed Sacrament, she heard the voice of her Savior. His voice was loud and clear in the silence of her heart. 'Begin to write,' He said."[74]

Among the records supporting these miracles can also be found stories of other visions and voices which come from the Eucharist. Examples include cases in which a 'saint' is allowed to see visions of paradise or of angels, or even the bodily appearance of Jesus at various stages of His life. One such vision occurred in the 16th century to Catherine of Jesus while she was adoring the Blessed Sacrament. During the vision she heard 'heavenly voices' singing the words of Revelation 7:12.[75]

Whether they involve speaking hosts, bleeding hosts, or levitating hosts, all of these miracles are believed to provide vital evidence of the True Presence of Jesus Christ in the Eucharist. And the Catholic Church has testified to the veracity of the miracles; it is a fact that many of those miracles mentioned above

---

[73] Lord, *This is My Body, This is My Blood: Miracles of the Eucharist, Book II*, pp. 228-9. I must note that Mother Angelica may or may not have understood this as an audible voice. She does not make this clear in her statement. Nonetheless, whatever she heard, whether inwardly or audibly, she heard while adoring and praying to the Eucharist. In whatever way she experienced it, this much is clear: the host spoke to her.

[74] *To Bear Witness*, pg. 38, para. 22

[75] Cruz, pp. 251-5

played an important role in elevating the respective visionaries to the status of Venerable, Blessed or Saint. These miracles are believed to testify to the piety of the people who experienced them, and though the approval of the miracles of the speaking Eucharist is given indirectly by the Catholic Church, it is given nonetheless.

These miracles of speaking hosts, like those which involve blood, are purported to testify to the Roman Catholic doctrine of the Presence of Jesus' Body, Blood, Soul and Divinity in the bread. If He is present and bleeding in the host, then it is no strange thing for Him also to speak to the faithful who worship Him there. But these miracles are significant for a different reason than the mere fact that they very effectively complement the miracles involving blood. These events which involve the speaking host are closely linked with the apparitions of Mary, as the Fowler, Abóbora and de la Roche miracles, above, clearly demonstrate. And more importantly, the miracles indicate that the Eucharist, which the apparitions of Mary have erected for worship in honor of the papacy, has not only been brought to life through the issuing of blood, but has been given the power of speech as well.

Pour encourager les autres...

> Can unjust judges be your allies,
> those who create burdens in the name of law,
> Those who conspire against the just and condemn
> the innocent to death?
> --*Psalm 94:20-21*

THERE is an office in Rome where the truth of Catholicism is kept pure, a place where true doctrine is kept free from all contamination of error and heresy. This office has been used for centuries to assure that nothing but the true Catholic faith is passed on to the next generation of Christians. At the present time it is called the Sacred Congregation for the Doctrine of the Faith. Five hundred years ago it was called the Holy Office of the Inquisition. The Office of the Inquisition was never disbanded--just renamed.

Many authors have written of the Inquisitions and their impact on history. Whether it be Turberville's *The Spanish Inquisition,* a somewhat favorable account of the diligence and courage of the Papacy, or Llorente's *A Critical History of the Inquisition of Spain,* which casts the Inquisitions in a negative light, they all agree on one thing: the Inquisitions are a blemish on the history of the Church. No one disputes the horrors of the Tribunals and no one would deny that Innocent IV's Bull of May 15, 1252, gave official Vatican approval for the use of torture in extracting confessions from unrepentant heretics.[76] These are all historical facts that neither Protestants nor Catholics deny.

---

[76] Pope Innocent IV, Papal Bull *Ad Extirpanda de Medio Populi*

continued on next page

Therefore, I do not wish to expound on the excruciating methods of torture used by the Inquisitors. That has already been thoroughly studied by historians and I prefer not to duplicate their efforts. By avoiding that topic I do not wish to ignore its importance, but rather to attempt to move beyond it and establish something much more critical to our understanding of what the tribunals of the Inquisitions were all about. Juan Antonio Llorente put it well when he said,

> "I shall not describe the different modes of torture employed by the Inquisition, as it has been already done by many historians: I shall only say that none of them can be accused of exaggeration."[77]

Even Catholic scholar Richard P. McBrien, in his exhaustive two volume work, *Catholicism*, touches only briefly on the subject of the Inquisitions by acknowledging Innocent IV's approval of torture "to secure proof of heresy," and then concedes the obvious: "By all reasonable standards, the Inquisition was one of the shabbiest chapters in the entire history of the Church."[78] So I need not dwell on the inhumanities that were practiced during this time of human history. Protestants and Catholics know it all too well and both parties willfully agree, albeit to varying degrees, that the Inquisitions were a poor reflection on the Catholic hierarchy. This much is without question.

What I *do* wish to emphasize about the Holy Inquisition, however, is the fact that the Eucharist was at the very center of it. It is a well-kept secret of history that the worship of the Eucharist was once considered the indication of a true Christian, and that refusal to bow before the Eucharist was considered the mark of a heretic. Such heretics were at the mercy of the Tribunals of the Inquisition. So while the tortures of the Inquisitors will not be

---

Christiani Pravitatis Zizania, May 15, 1252. *The Cambridge Medieval History*, Volume VI: Victory of the Papacy, (Cambridge University Press, ©1964) pg. 725

[77] Llorente, Juan Antonio, *A Critical History of the Inquisition of Spain*, (Williamstown, MA: The John Lilburne Company, Publishers, ©1967. First English translation, 1823) pg. 65

[78] McBrien, Richard P., *Catholicism*, volume 2, (MN: Winston Press, ©1980) pg. 623

addressed here, their mandate to bow before and worship the bread of the altar will be.

The Eucharist has long held an exalted position in the liturgy of the Catholic Church. In fact, just participating in the Sacrifice of the Mass is, in and of itself, a form of worshipping the Eucharist. Pope John Paul II has confirmed this understanding by writing in 1980,

> "...the church has always required from the faithful respect and reverence for the eucharist at the moment of receiving it... 'When the faithful communicate (receive communion) kneeling, no other sign of reverence toward the Blessed Sacrament is required, since kneeling is itself a sign of adoration.'"[79]

Thus, one renders adoration, or worship, to the Eucharistic Christ merely by receiving the wafer during communion.

This practice is universal among Catholics. To this day they are still instructed to genuflect on one knee, or bow, toward the Eucharist upon entering the church building. And though the Roman Church has come a long way in recognizing the rights of those Christians who are unwilling to show such reverence to the bread of the altar, the simple fact remains that those who do bow to the bread are in reality worshipping it whether they ever knew it or not--because that is what the Catholic Church teaches to, and requires of, its faithful. In the past, those who refused to bow before the Eucharist or refused to attend Mass, according to historical records, have been put to death. Of course we are not presently living in such times, but during the 15th century--and for several which preceded it--Christians were put to death for refusing to worship the bread of the altar. Thus, there was a time when the mere presence of the Eucharist demanded and received such respect from those who were willing to give it.

---

[79] Pope John Paul II, Instruction *Inæstimabile Donum,* Sacred Congregation for the Sacraments and Divine Worship: "On Certain Norms Concerning Worship of the Eucharistic Mystery," section A, The Mass, article 11. John Paul II quotes from the Sacred Congregation of Rites, instruction *Eucharisticum Mysterium*, 34. Parentheses added for clarity

It was on that specific point that many Protestants parted from Catholicism, and even in France, where no official papal inquisition was ever established, the Catholic clergy and laity still insisted on weeding out heresy by the most intimidating methods. And the doctrine of the Eucharist was the central issue of any inquiry. Martin Luther's teachings on justification by faith alone and *sola scriptura* created enough of a stir in 1519 to cause the faculty of theology at the University of Paris to condemn them within two years. The prohibition against Luther's teachings soon extended to all religious writings so that no one could publish a religious book without first obtaining permission from the faculty of theology.[80] This gradually led to more and more restrictions against non-Catholics, and the king soon found that his role in preserving truth was somewhat diminished in light of the assumed powers of the University of Paris, which sought above all else to preserve the Roman Catholic doctrine of the Eucharist:

> "Although the king was willing and able to protect individuals when their views seemed to him orthodox, the growing scale of Protestantism in France and the assault on a number of doctrines that Francis I held to be absolutely essential to religious orthodoxy--*notably the doctrine of the Eucharist*--diminished the king's role over the next several decades and heightened that of *parlement* and the faculty of theology at Paris. The king himself appears to have followed the custom in France since the late thirteenth century of appointing an inquisitor-general from the Dominican Order."[81]

From France to Spain to anywhere else that the inquisition manifested itself, the Eucharist was the central theme and was considered the doctrine most worthy of defense. Miles Phillips, a prisoner of the Spanish Inquisitions from 1568 to 1575, gives a personal account of his experience with the Tribunals. In the following entry in his diary, he describes how his very life depended on whether or not he would acknowledge the Catholic doctrine of transubstantiation, or the True Presence of Jesus in the Eucharist:

---

[80] Peters, Edward, *Inquisition*, (New York: The Free Press, a division of Macmillan, Inc., ©1988) pg. 141

[81] Peters, pp. 141-2. Emphasis added

> "During which time of our imprisonment... we were often called before the Inquisitors alone; and there severely examined of our faith... Then did they proceed to demand of us, upon our oaths, 'What we did believe of the Sacrament?' and 'Whether there did remain any bread or wine, after the words of consecration, Yea or No?' and 'Whether we did not believe that the Host of bread which the priest did hold up over his head, and the wine that was in the chalice, was the very true and perfect body and blood of our Saviour Christ, Yea or No?' *To which, if we answered not 'Yea!' then there was no way but death*."[82]

Miles Phillip's account was not the exception. It was the order of the day. Protestants were killed regularly for refusing to attend Mass to worship the Eucharist. This is not to emphasize their deaths, but rather to emphasize precisely what preceded them. The Eucharist was the center of the controversy:

> "Jacob Birone, a schoolmaster of Rorata, for refusing to change his religion, was stripped quite naked ...and was led through the streets with a soldier on each side of him. At every turning the soldier on his right hand side cut a gash in his flesh, and the soldier on his left hand side struck him with a bludgeon, both saying, at the same instant, '*Will you go to Mass? will you go to Mass?*' He still replied in the negative to these interrogatories, and being at length taken to the bridge, they cut off his head on the balustrades, and threw both that and his body into the river."[83]

It is during the Mass that the transformation of the bread and wine takes place. Likewise, it is during the Mass that the faithful adore the bread--which was what Birone was being asked to do. Transubstantiation, and the worship which follows, were the key doctrines of the Inquisition, and many a Christian lost his life for refusing to give the bread the honor which the Inquisitors reserved for it. During one particular confrontation between the Inquisitors and a group of Christians called the Waldenses, it was

---

[82] *Eyewitness to History*, John Carey, ed., (Cambridge, MA: Harvard University Press, ©1987) pg. 112. Emphasis added

[83] Fox, John, *Fox's Book of Martyrs*, (Grand Rapids, MI: Zondervan Publishing House, ©1926,1954,1967), Forbush, William Byron, D.D., ed., pp. 110-1. Emphasis added

determined by a council at Turin, and under the authority of Pope Paul III, that the following proposition be made:

> "That if the Waldenses would come to the bosom of the Church of Rome, and embrace the Roman Catholic religion, they should enjoy their houses, properties, and lands, and live with their families, without the least molestation."[84]

The offer was finally presented to the Waldenses, guaranteeing them "...that they should receive no injury, if they would accept of preachers appointed by the pope; but if they would not, they should be deprived both of their properties and lives." When the Waldenses refused, they were ordered "to attend Mass regularly on pain of death."[85] Indeed, since attending Mass and receiving the bread is a form of worshipping the Eucharist according to the teachings of Pope John Paul II, the Waldenses were killed for refusing to adore the bread of the altar and participate in the Eucharistic Sacrifice.

Likewise, a man named Daniel Rambaut was also put to death for refusing to accept the Catholic doctrines on the Eucharist. Again, it is clear that his refusal to honor or worship the Eucharist was the cause of his death:

> "Daniel Rambaut, of Vilario, the father of a numerous family, was ...told that he might yet save his life, if he would subscribe to the belief of the following articles:
>
> 1. *The real presence of the host*, 2. *Transubstantiation*, 3. Purgatory, 4. The pope's infallibility, 5. *That Masses for the dead will release souls from Purgatory*, 6. That praying to the saints will procure the remission of sins...
>
> "The priests were so highly offended at M. Rambaut's answers ...that they determined to shake his resolution by the most cruel method imaginable... but finding that he bore his sufferings with the most admirable patience, increased both in fortitude and resignation, and maintained his faith with steadfast resolution and unshaken constancy they stabbed him to the heart, and then gave his body to be devoured by the dogs."[86]

---

[84] Fox, pg. 96

[85] Fox, pg. 90, 97

[86] Fox, pp. 113-4. Emphasis added

Rawlins White was yet another victim of the Inquisitions as his refusal to worship the Eucharist resulted in his death, as well:

> "After this, the bishop tried what saying Mass would do; but Rawlins called all the people to witness *that he did not bow down to the host.* Mass being ended, Rawlins was called for again; to whom the bishop used many persuasions; but …the bishop's discourse was to no purpose. …In about three weeks the order came from town for his (Rawlins') execution."[87]

Peter Spengler, another victim of the Tribunals, was killed because he would not accept the doctrine of transubstantiation and would not worship the Eucharist by attending Mass:

> "Peter Spengler… of the town of Schalet, was thrown into the river, and drowned. Before he was taken to the banks of the stream which was to become his grave, they led him to the market place that his crimes might be proclaimed; which were, *not going to Mass*, not making confession, and *not believing in transubstantiation*."[88]

One Christian man named Sharpe gave in to the pressures of the Inquisitors and confessed that the bread and wine were truly the Body, Blood, Soul and Divinity of Jesus. Later he recanted during Mass, denying the doctrines to which he had converted under duress, and was burned to death for it. The key issue, of course, is not that he was burned to death, but that his death was the punishment meted out for refusing to worship the bread:

> "Mr. Sharpe, weaver, of Bristol, was brought the ninth day of March, 1556, before Dr. Dalby, chancellor of the city of Bristol, and after examination concerning the Sacrament of the altar, was persuaded to recant; and on the twenty-ninth, he was enjoined to make his recantation in the parish church. But, scarcely had he publicly avowed his backsliding, before he felt in his conscience such a tormenting fiend, that he was unable to work at his occupation; hence, shortly after, one Sunday, he came into the parish church, called Temple, and after high Mass, stood up in the choir door, and said with a loud voice, 'Neighbors, bear me record that yonder idol

---

[87] Fox, pg. 222. Parentheses added for clarity, emphasis added

[88] Fox, pg. 168. Emphasis added

(pointing to the altar) is the greatest and most abominable that ever was; and I am sorry that I ever denied my Lord God!' ...Shortly after, before the chancellor, *denying the Sacrament of the altar to be the body and blood of Christ*, he was condemned to be burned by Mr. Dalby."[89]

It was unfortunate that some who were subjected to the Tribunals did indeed recant and profess belief in the doctrines of the Eucharist, but a simple recantation was not enough. The accused was not allowed to rest in death until he had publicly requested that the Eucharist be administered to him in person. Llorente writes,

"If the accused was repentant, and demanded to be reconciled after having relapsed, he was to be delivered over to secular justice, and was destined to suffer capital punishment. The inquisitors, after having passed judgment on him, engaged some priests, who were in their confidence, to inform him of his situation, and induce him to demand the sacrament of penance and the communion."[90]

And since receiving communion, according to the doctrines of the Catholic Church, is an act of worshipping the bread, and is a public expression of assent to the doctrine of transubstantiation, it can be properly asserted that a 'convert' was required immediately to worship the bread. This is not mere conjecture. It is the expressed belief of the Magisterium of the Catholic Church.

While the Eucharist was the central focus of the Tribunals of the Inquisition, it was also central to the administration of the death sentences of the unrepentant. When a convicted heretic was to be burned, the members of the local town or city were required to participate in the burning as an *auto da fé*--an act of faith:

"After judgment, a procession is performed to the place of execution, which ceremony is called an *auto da fé*, or act of faith. The following is an account of an *auto da fé*, performed at Madrid in the year 1682: ...Mass began, in the midst of which the priest came from the altar, placed himself near the scaffold, and seated himself in a chair prepared for that

---

[89] Fox, pg. 279. Parentheses in original, emphasis added
[90] Llorente, pg. 28

> purpose. The chief inquisitor then descended from the amphitheater, dressed in his cope, and having a miter on his head. After having bowed to the altar, he advanced towards the king's balcony, and went up to it, attended by some of his officers, carrying a cross and the Gospels... The Mass was begun about twelve at noon, and did not end until nine in the evening, being protracted by a proclamation of the sentences of the several criminals, which were already separately rehearsed aloud one after the other."[91]

The key point in the preceding quote is not that the heretics were burned alive (as is well known), but rather that the celebration of High Mass, the participation in the worship of the Eucharistic Mystery, was the central event in their death sentence.

Without dwelling unnecessarily on the torturous methods of examination and execution, then, it is enough to say that the Eucharist was indeed central to the purpose and procedure of the Inquisitions. Central also to the administration of the Tribunals was the confiscation of goods from the accused, as the inquisition against the Waldenses (above, pg. 58) clearly demonstrates. These confiscated goods, if of any value, were used to maintain the tremendous overhead expenses of operating the Tribunals.[92] By confiscating finances and properties, the tribunals also assured that whoever was guilty of failing to adore the Eucharist was also unable to participate in any financial exchange with his business partners, and of course was rendered unable to purchase basic necessities to sustain a family. For all purposes, an accused heretic was denied the ability to buy or sell goods, services and properties if he refused to acknowledge and worship the True Physical Presence of Jesus Christ in the Eucharist:

> "The sentence of the Inquisition imposed a variety of fines and personal penalties, such as entire or partial confiscation; perpetual, or a limited period of imprisonment; exile, or transportation; infamy, and the loss of employments, honours, and dignities."[93]

---

[91] Fox, pg. 62. Italics in original

[92] Roth, Cecil, M.A., Ph.D., Oxon., *The Spanish Inquisition*, (New York: W.W. Norton & Company, Inc., ©1964) pg. 37

[93] Llorente, pg. 29

"A defence in the Inquisition is of little use to the prisoner, for a suspicion only is deemed sufficient cause for condemnation, and the greater his wealth the greater his danger."[94]

"At a further *auto [da fé]* of December 22, 1560, there were fourteen relaxations* in person and three in effigy... Among the other persons relaxed were two Englishmen, named Brooks and Burton respectively. The latter was a ship's captain. All the merchandise on board his vessel was forfeited, and, when another Englishman, named Frampton, was sent out to endeavour to recover the property he not only failed in his mission, but fell into the hands of the Inquisition. As the result of severe torture he promised to embrace Roman Catholicism."[95]

We need not dwell overly long on the fact that the Inquisitors imposed financial sanctions on, and then confiscated the properties of, those who refused to honor the Eucharist. It is sufficient to say that the interrogating official of the Tribunal was called "the procurator-fiscal,"[96] a word which necessarily implies financial seizure and intimidation. The central theme of the Inquisitions was the Eucharist, and the punishments consistently were fiscal and economic restrictions, and death by various means for those who refused to bow to the bread of the altar. This was so well known by the general populace of the time that the mere mention of the Inquisitors, or the Tribunals over which they presided, struck fear into the hearts of the nobility and common people alike. The Inquisitors had become so thorough in their dealings that they gained for the Eucharist a certain respect and fear among the people--a respect that would have otherwise been reserved for some of history's most infamous dictators:

---

94 Fox, pg. 61

* Relaxation is a euphemism for 'extermination.' The word was used commonly to describe the death of an impenitent heretic and should not be taken to mean 'acquittal,' which is what 'relaxation' would normally seem to imply

95 Turberville, Arthur Stanley, *The Spanish Inquisition*, (Oxford University Press: Archon Books, ©1932) pg. 139. Brackets added for clarity

96 Llorente, pp. 64-5

> "By the end of the thirteenth century, it (the Inquisition) had developed a system of great thoroughness, with a hierarchy of officials and detailed records, and its arm was notoriously long, so that the very name already struck terror into every wavering heart. It had attained complete independence, and had the support of secular authority, by which its introduction had generally been welcomed; it possessed its own prisons; and it wrapped all its affairs in inviolable secrecy."[97]

> "Courts of Inquisition were now erected in several countries; but the Spanish Inquisition became the most powerful, and the most dreaded of any. Even the kings of Spain themselves, though arbitrary in all other respects, were taught to dread the power of the lords of the Inquisition; and the horrid cruelties they exercised compelled multitudes, who differed in opinion from the Roman Catholics, carefully to conceal their sentiments."[98]

Indeed, kings, queens and other royalty were not only invited to participate in the executions. They were required by oath to do so. Whenever a European king or queen ascended to the throne, he or she was required to swear by oath to enforce the sentences of the Tribunals:

> "The king's near situation to the criminals rendered their dying groans very audible to him; he could not, however, be absent from this dreadful scene, as it is esteemed a religious one; and his coronation oath obliged him to give a sanction by his presence to all the acts of the tribunal."[99]

Whether of noble birth or common, the Eucharist struck fear into the heart of everyone. No person, whether great or small, poor or rich, was without fear that the Tribunals might seek him out next and force him to bow to the bread of the altar.

All of the financial and physical punishments notwithstanding, there is another thread which runs commonly through the Tribunals of the Inquisitions: the apparitions of Mary. It is interesting that Miles Phillips, in his diary written during his

---

[97] Roth, pg. 37. Parentheses added for clarity

[98] Fox, pg. 60

[99] Fox, pp. 62-3

imprisonment, also recorded that apparitions of Mary were locally active at the time of his incarceration. In describing the time period and the circumstances of his arrest, Phillips wrote that,

> "...every year, upon our Lady's Day, the people use to repair thither to offer, and to pray in the church before the image: and they say that Our Lady of Guadaloupe doth work a number of miracles."[100]

And at the same time that the Inquisitions were raging in Europe, the apparitions of Mary were occurring regularly both in Europe and in the New World.

> "One of the greatest apparitions in Church history occurred when the Blessed Virgin appeared to Juan Diego at Guadalupe, Mexico in 1531. Within a time span of fifty years or so there were numerous accounts of the other Marian apparitions in Mexico which helped Christianity spread throughout the Americas."[101]

The apparitions of the 16th century assisted the Conquistadors in conquering the new world but never once admonished them for their inhumane methods of forced conversion, and without once admonishing the popes for blessing the efforts. And all the while on the other side of the Atlantic there was a slaughter taking place which the apparitions not only knew about but failed to admonish either by word or deed. The tortures of the 16th century are widely known, but there is something equally significant which is not as well understood: during that time, the apparitions of Mary played an important part in perpetuating the doctrine of bowing to the Eucharist, and did so at a time when the Inquisitions were at the peak of their ferocity.

The apparition of course did not care to stop the slaughter, for many of the tortures of the Inquisition were performed in its name. The apparitions were central to the Inquisitions, just as the Eucharist was, and Mary's name was often invoked to encourage a heretic to repent. The Inquisition against William Lithgow gives evidence of this:

---

[100] *Eyewitness to History*, pg. 109

[101] *A Call to Peace*, Volume 4, Number 2, "The Age of Marian Apparitions," pp. 1,15-17

> "One of the Jesuits said, (first making the sign of the cross upon his breast), 'My son, behold, you deserve to be burnt alive; but by the grace of our lady of Loretto, whom you have blasphemed we will both save your soul and body.' ...'Convert, convert, O dear brother, for our blessed Lady's sake convert!'"[102]

Miles Philipps' appearance before the Tribunals provides evidence of the exalted position of Marian devotion in the minds of the Inquisitors as well. He states that in addition to being asked if he believed in transubstantiation of the Eucharist, he was also instructed to recite the Our Father, the Hail Mary, and the Apostles' Creed, which are three of the primary prayers of the Rosary, a form of devotion which has its origins in the apparitions of Mary:

> "During which time of our imprisonment... we were often called before the Inquisitors alone... and commanded to say the *Pater noster* (Our Father), the *Ave Maria* (Hail Mary), and the *Creed*, in Latin: which, God knoweth! a great number of us could not say otherwise than in the English tongue."[103]

Even to the present day, the apparitions of Mary have applauded the efforts of the Papacy in maintaining true doctrine. Don Stephano Gobbi, an itinerant locutionist and Catholic priest, recently received messages from the apparition of Mary which lauded the historical efforts of the Papacy in preserving the truth:

> "A true reunification of Christians is not possible unless it be in the perfection of truth. And truth has been kept intact only in the Catholic Church, which must preserve it, defend it and proclaim it to all without fear. ...the authentic Magisterium of the Church has always taught and energetically defended against any heretical deviation whatsoever."[104]

---

[102] Fox, pp. 82-3. Parentheses in original

[103] *Eyewitness to History*, pg. 112. Italics in original, parentheses added for clarity

[104] *Our Lady Queen of Peace*, "Jesus to the World: My mother must be heard in the totality of her messages," pg. 18, and "Interior Locutions," pg. 6. Messages of October 27, 1980 and June 11, 1988, respectively. Used by permission

There were no apologies for not coming to the aid of the Protestant 'heretics' during the Inquisitions, and no admonition to the Papacy for approving the use of force and torture to extract confessions from the accused. Just a simple affirmation of the truth that has been preserved by the Catholic Church throughout history, and an unspoken approval of the methods that were used to do it.

It was by these methods, according to the absolute power granted by the Papacy, and by the authority of the apparitions of Mary, that the Inquisitors could deliver on such fearsome threats as to make aristocrats and peasants alike tremble at the mention of the Eucharist. Because of this, few were without fear of the Inquisition, and no segment of society was immune to its effects. In his *Book of Martyrs,* John Fox describes the extent of the Inquisition's effects and its reputation:

> "...the maxim of the Inquisition being to strike terror, and awe those who are the objects of its power into obedience. High birth, distinguished rank, great dignity, or eminent employments, are no protection from its severities; and the lowest officers of the Inquisition can make the highest characters tremble."[105]

In this manner, fear was driven into the hearts of all who knew of the Eucharist, this Sacrament of the Altar. Their rights were withheld, their properties confiscated, and not surprisingly, their ability to transact business was severely restricted. No one who refused to honor the Eucharist could, at the same time, maintain the freedom to engage openly in business. And as the inquisition against the sea merchant Frampton (above, pg. 62) clearly illustrates, even the nonreligious mind was more than happy to accept the doctrines of Eucharistic worship if for no other reason than to retain the privilege of continuing financial transactions. And, as the inquisition against the Waldenses makes clear (above, pg. 58), the first phase of intimidation was to threaten to seize property. It is a fact that the Eucharist was the determining factor, and the right to buy and sell, and indeed, to live, was the privilege that was in the balance. And whether or not a person believed the doctrines of the Catholic Church, he was

[105] Fox, pg. 61

often willing to convert solely because of what was known to happen to those who refused.

Worship of the Eucharist and the doctrine of the True Physical Presence were the central issues of the Inquisitions, and the apparitions of Mary played their part in supporting them. Since then, the apparitions of Mary have acknowledged and even approved of--if only by their silence--the procedures by which the Inquisitions were perpetuated. The Papacy allowed the use of torture during the Inquisitions as a means of preserving true doctrine, and the apparitions of Mary applauded the efforts. All emotional issues aside, one cannot deny the historical evidence which clearly demonstrates that the apparitions of Mary, though active in the many localities where the Tribunals were in session, did nothing to counter the effects of the forced worship of the bread of the altar.

By failing to do so, the apparitions honored the doctrines of the Papacy and became responsible for forcing people to bow down to worship the Eucharist which had been brought to life and had been given the power of speech. And regardless of whether people today believe that the Inquisitions were good or necessary, one cannot escape the fact that the Eucharist was the central issue, and that people feared it. Those who did not lost life, limb and property.

Part 2: Handmaid

My soul proclaims the greatness of the
Lord;
my spirit rejoices in God my savior.
For he has looked upon his handmaid's
lowliness;
behold, from now on will all ages
call me blessed.
The Mighty One has done great things
for me,
and holy is his name.

--Luke 1:46-49

Authority to Proceed

Then he summoned his twelve disciples and gave them authority...

--*Matthew 10:1a*

ALTHOUGH the tradition of the Catholic Church has long held that Mary the mother of Jesus was sinless, it was not until the 1850s that the Papacy first proclaimed an official doctrine to that effect. And though the Bible had never spoken clearly of Mary's complete innocence before God, Pope Pius IX, in his 1854 Bull *Ineffabilis Deus*, proclaimed that Mary had been conceived without sin and henceforth was to be called the Immaculate Conception. That is, he declared that she was completely free of the sinful nature that is common to man. Ninety-six years later, Pope Pius XII would continue what Pius IX had started. Having proclaimed that Mary was without sin, it was only a small step for the Papacy to proclaim that Mary had been assumed, or taken body and soul, into Heaven when her earthly life was complete. And in his 1950 Apostolic Constitution *Munificentissimus Deus,* Pope Pius XII proclaimed exactly that.

I say 'small step' because the new doctrine regarding the Assumption of Mary rested on the authority of the Immaculate Conception doctrine. In fact, it is safe to say that the Assumption doctrine followed logically from the Immaculate Conception and served as a natural complement to it. Pius XII reasoned that if death was sin's consequence, and if Mary was without sin, then Mary would have escaped the effects of sin: death and bodily decay. As one theologian concluded, it was thoroughly illogical to suppose that Mary, having carried the sinless savior in her womb, should ever be subject to death's curse: 'unto dust thou shalt return.'[106] That being the case, the only other option was that Mary had been assumed into heaven without ever tasting the consequences of sin. This is known as the doctrine of the Assumption of Mary and includes the little known precept that upon Mary's arrival in Heaven, she was crowned Queen of Heaven and Earth.[107] This last notion, generally disagreeable to Protestants who know of it, has long been celebrated by Catholics in the form of the prayers of the Rosary. In fact, the last ten Hail Marys of a complete Rosary are reserved entirely for meditation upon this very Mystery: that Mary, having received her dominion from the Father, Son and Spirit, now dispenses Their graces from her exalted throne in Heaven.

As I said, Protestants who are familiar with it are generally troubled by the notion, but they need not provide excuses for such feelings. Scripture has made no mention of any such exaltation of Mary, and neither does it refer to her innocence. None of the apostles ever mentioned such a position being reserved for Mary in Heaven, and none of them suggested that anyone but Christ Himself was without sin. Protestants need not feel any remorse in completely disagreeing with the doctrines of Mary; and, were it not for the requirement that they believe them, Catholics would be free to dispense with these doctrines as well. The dogma of the Assumption of Mary was in fact made a matter of *fides catholica*, or obligatory faith, by Pope Pius XII when he proclaimed the doctrine in 1950,[108] just as Pius IX had done when he proclaimed the doctrine of the Immaculate Conception in 1854.[109]

But there is something peculiar about these Catholic Marian doctrines. Since the doctrines allowed for Mary to be without sin, and therefore required that she not experience bodily corruption, they likewise indicated that Mary has enjoyed something in which most dead people have not yet shared: the bodily resurrection. When Pius XII defined the doctrine of the Assumption of Mary, he made this point especially clear:

---

[106] Lonergan, Bernard J. F., "The Dogma of the Assumption," 1st in a series of 5 radio broadcasts, November 1950, Broadcast I: "The Ensign," 1. (Duggan, pg. 18)

[107] Pius XII, *Munificentissimus Deus*, AAS 42(1950):762

[108] Pius XII, *Munificentissimus Deus*, AAS 42(1950):770

[109] Pius IX, *Ineffabilis Deus*, (1854)

> "Yet, according to the general rule, God does not will to grant to the just the full effect of the victory over death until the end of time has come. And so it is that the bodies of even the just are corrupted after death, and only on the last day will they be joined, each to its own glorious soul. Now God has willed that the Blessed Virgin Mary should be exempt from this general rule. She, by an entirely unique privilege, completely overcame sin by her Immaculate Conception, and as a result she was not subject to the law of remaining in the corruption of the grave, and she did not have to wait until the end of time for the redemption of her body."[110]

When Pope Pius XII defined the doctrine of the Assumption of Mary, he made it perfectly clear that since Mary had been made exempt from the rule of bodily corruption, she is therefore the only human in Heaven who presently enjoys the benefits of the physical resurrection. By establishing the Assumption, the Papacy made it logically possible for Mary to appear in her bodily form; this means that if Mary were so inclined, she could appear to people on earth, and she could do so, not as a mere spirit, but as the resurrected, glorified, physical Mary. The conditional clause here is important: *if Mary were so inclined.*

Of course, Mary has not been inclined to do any such thing, but something masquerading as Mary has done exactly that. Something has been appearing *bodily* as the glorified, resurrected Mary for over one thousand years, always reaffirming the authority of the Papacy, and likewise encouraging the people of the world to submit to the teachings of the Pope. I am speaking of course of the many occurrences of the apparitions or visions of Mary which have already been discussed, and I do not wish to argue about whether or not Mary could appear if she wanted to. The point I wish to bring out is not that Mary can or cannot appear bodily from Heaven, but the fact that the apparitions claim to do so by the authority of the Papacy. And though Protestants who are aware of the apparitions of Mary, and Catholics who follow them, do not agree on their origins, they would both certainly concede that, if true, the papal doctrines make the appearances a logical possibility.

---

110 Pius XII, *Munificentissimus Deus*, AAS 42(1950):754-755

These apparitions have indeed relied heavily on papal authority, and it would be a terrific understatement merely to say that the Papacy has enjoyed a very affectionate relationship with them. For example, in 1946, four years before Pope Pius XII proclaimed the doctrine of the Assumption of Mary, he "crowned her Queen of the World"[111] by placing a $500,000 crown on a statue of Mary at Fátima, Portugal,[112] a site known world-wide for the apparitions which occurred there in 1917. Pope John Paul II is also known for his devotion to Mary, and has rekindled that same devotion among Catholics by his many pilgrimages to various apparition sites. In 1979, he made a pilgrimage to Knock, Ireland, to commemorate the 100th anniversary of the apparitions there.[113] He also went on pilgrimage to Fátima, Portugal, in 1982,[114] and then visited Lourdes, France, the following year to honor the apparitions that had occurred there in 1858.[115] And regarding the still officially unapproved apparitions at Medjugorje, Pope John Paul II had this to say: "If I wasn't a Pope I'd be in Medjugorje already!"[116]

The apparitions of Mary have responded to this affection in kind by assisting the Papacy in times of trouble. For example, when Pope Pius IX proclaimed the doctrine of the Immaculate Conception in 1854, there was some concern among the Catholic clergy that the doctrine would not be well received by the general Catholic population. However, the apparition of Mary put these fears to rest when it appeared in Lourdes, France, in 1858 with the

---

[111] *Blue Army Cell Manual*, ©AMI Press, Blue Army of Our Lady of Fátima, Washington, New Jersey, 07882, pg. 3

[112] Haffert, John M., *Russia Will Be Converted*, (Washington, NJ: AMI International Press, ©1950) pp. 116-7

[113] Lord, Bob & Penny, *The Many Faces of Mary: A Love Story*, (Westlake Village, CA: Journeys of Faith, ©1987) pp. 125-6

[114] Zimdars-Swartz, Sandra L., *Encountering Mary*, (New York: Princeton University Press, ©1991) pg. 217

[115] Duggan, Paul E., *The Assumption Dogma: Some Reactions and Ecumenical Implications in the Thought of English-Speaking Theologians*, (Dayton, OH: International Marian Research Institute, ©1989) pp. 152-4

[116] Ashton, Joan, *The People's Madonna*, (London: Harper-Collins Publishers, ©1991) pg. 216

salutation, "I am the Immaculate Conception," thus confirming the doctrine that Pius IX had recently proclaimed. No apparition up to that time had ever referred to itself in that manner, and in so doing, the apparition put an end to the concerns of the Catholic clergy.[117]

Twelve years later, just before Pope Pius IX introduced the doctrine of Papal Infallibility at Vatican Council I in 1870, he received a message from visionary John Bosco who had received a message from the apparition of Mary. Apparently, 'she' wanted Pius IX to go forward with the proclamation of the Infallibility doctrine, and would help him at every step.[118] The doctrine was accepted with tremendous success at the first Vatican Council, just as the apparition had promised. Then, in 1950 when Pope Pius XII proclaimed the doctrine of the Assumption of Mary, he did so by appealing to the two doctrines that the Marian apparitions had helped Pius IX establish: the Immaculate Conception of Mary and the Infallibility of the Pope. In the preamble to the proclamation of the new dogma, Pius XII referred both to Mary, who was "immaculate in her conception," and to the authority of the Papacy, which was "infallibly" directed to proclaim such a doctrine.[119] The Assumption therefore rested on two very significant pillars that the apparition had helped erect, pillars which simultaneously demanded the proclamation of the dogma and made the proclamation possible: Mary was assumed into Heaven *because* she was immaculate, and the Papacy could proclaim the Assumption *because* it was infallible. Thus, the doctrines that made it possible for Mary to appear bodily from Heaven were influenced by the very apparitions that needed the doctrines in order to make their appearances.

And scarcely had the Papacy proclaimed the doctrine of the Assumption than the apparition began a new campaign to define the final Marian dogma. The apparition of Mary in Amsterdam on November 15, 1951, insisted to visionary Ida Peederman that it was time for the Church "to go further than it had yet gone. In

---

[117] Marnham, Patrick, *Lourdes: A Modern Pilgrimage*, (New York: Coward, McCann & Geoghegan, Inc., ©1980) pp. 4-9

[118] *Dreams, Visions & Prophecies of Don Bosco*, Brown, Eugene M., editor, (New Rochelle, NY: Don Bosco Publications, ©1986) pg. 114

[119] Pope Pius XII, *Munificentissimus Deus*, AAS 42(1950):769

these last days, with the forces of Satan gathering to do battle with Mary and her followers, it was time... for the Church to proclaim her, as she had asked, 'Co-Redemptrix, Mediatrix, and Advocate.'"[120] It has not taken long for faithful Catholics to respond. In fact, one of the most notable proponents of the doctrine is Mother Teresa herself, who says, "The papal definition of Mary as Coredemptrix, Mediatrix, and Advocate will bring great graces to the Church."[121] If Mother Teresa's aid in establishing the doctrine is not sufficient, then John Paul II's own theological advisor will certainly lend his support, for it is he who wrote the foreword for a recent book advising John Paul II to proceed steadfastly with the proclamation of the new doctrine.[122]

By saying this I do not wish to criticize the proponents of the final doctrine, or any of those who adhere to the other doctrines, but rather to establish the much more critical point: that the apparitions of Mary have demonstrated in the past, and demonstrate in the present, that they need doctrines to be proclaimed *for* them. And they know exactly to whom they should go to get them: the Papacy. Indeed, any authority which the apparitions enjoy is received directly from Rome. The apparition's urgent plea from Amsterdam on November 15, 1951 (above, pg. 75) could hardly make that more clear.

If and when the final Marian doctrine is proclaimed, it will represent a most interesting series of characteristics attributed to Mary by the Papacy. When one considers the Marian doctrines by themselves, they seem to be rather odd, but nothing extraordinary in and of themselves. Just ordinarily Catholic. But place them together and they tell a different story.

We know that Jesus is our sinless Savior, and we know it for one very important reason: the Scriptures teach us this very thing.* Now the Catholic Church has taught that Mary is sinless as well. We know that Jesus necessarily rose from the dead in

---

[120] Zimdars-Swartz, pp. 257-8. Message of November 15, 1951

[121] *Signs of the Times*, Volume 5, Number 4, September/October/November 1993, "Marian News Update: Lay Group Seeks New Marian Dogma," pp. 6-7

[122] Miravalle, Mark I., S.T.D., *Mary: Coredemptrix, Mediatrix, Advocate*, (Santa Barbara, CA: Queenship Publishing, ©1993) pg. ix

* Hebrews 7:26

order to conquer death. Had He not risen, our faith would be empty, for that is also what the Scriptures teach us.* Now the Catholic Church has taught that Mary was resurrected from the dead as well (if she even died at all).† The traditional descriptions of her resurrection almost make Jesus' pale by comparison:

> "Is it true that the source of life, that the Mother of my Lord died? Yes because it was necessary that that which was of earth return to the earth, and be thus transported from earth to heaven, after having received immortal life... It was necessary that the incorruptible and immaculate flesh (of the Virgin) pass like gold through the crucible of death, to lay aside the opaque earthly mass of mortality and rise from the grave all radiant with the brightness of incorruptibility."[123]

This focus on Mary's resurrection is not without effect. For while Christians have long understood that Jesus' resurrection from the dead guarantees us a certain hope of our own future resurrection, Mary's resurrection is now believed to take the place of that. Her victory over the grave is purported to lend us the strength we need to persevere:

> "The Assumption is in fact a pressing invitation to faith in the resurrection of the body, to hope in life everlasting, and to charity, which is the indispensable condition for a glorious resurrection and happy eternal life... As Christ our Head is risen, as Mary, the neck of the Mystical Body, which unites all other members to the head, is risen, so must our bodies also rise and be reunited to their souls for participation in their eternal destiny."[124]

---

* 1 Corinthians 15:14

† In fact, this issue was never resolved at the highest levels of the Roman Catholic Church. The Apostolic Constitution *Munificentissimus Deus* makes no mention of Mary's death and avoids the topic altogether by saying that Mary was ascended into heaven "when the course of her earthly life was finished." (Pope Pius XII, *Munificentissimus Deus*, AAS 42(1950):77)

123 Damascene, John, *Encomium in Dormition*, Homily 3, 2-3, (Duggan, pg. 28). Parentheses in original

124 Roschini, "Assumption Proof given in Vatican Radio Lecture," *Catholic Action of the South* (1950),1. (Duggan, pg. 40)

Thus, just as Jesus' unique sinlessness has been transferred to Mary through the Immaculate Conception doctrine, so has the uniqueness of His Resurrection been transferred by the Assumption doctrine. And just as we are to endure this life because of His resurrection, we are now instructed by the Papacy to persevere because of Mary's. But the transfer of His attributes does not end there. The Scriptures teach us that Jesus is our Redeemer in that He suffered for us, our Mediator in that He intercedes for us, and our Advocate in that He defends us.* This is what the Scriptures teach us about Him and it is indeed the very reason we call Him Savior. But now the Papacy is on the verge of completing its array of Marian doctrines, the third of which will represent the complete transfer of messianic attributes from Jesus to Mary (see *Transfer of Messianic Attributes from Jesus to Mary*, below). Indeed, all of the attributes which make Jesus unique as Savior have been transferred--if not through the proclamation of new doctrines, then through Tradition--from Jesus Christ to Mary.

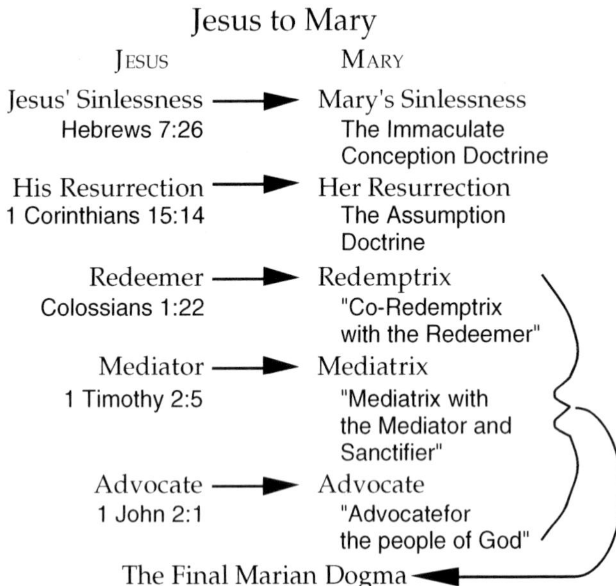

* Colossians 1:22, 1 Timothy 2:5, and 1 John 2:1

To say then that the Papacy has honored the apparitions would be an understatement. It has in fact done much more than that. It has made salvation possible through Mary, which is exactly what the apparitions needed. With the proclamation of the third Marian doctrine the transfer will be complete, for the apparition of Mary told visionary Ida Peederman that this would be the last Marian doctrine to be proclaimed:

> "It is as Co-Redemptrix and Mediatrix that I come at these times. I was Co-Redemptrix from the moment of the Annunciation. This is the meaning: the mother has been constituted Co-Redemptrix by the will of the Father. Tell this to your theologians. Tell them likewise that this dogma will be the last in Marian history."[125]

Why the last? Because that is all the apparition of Mary needs. And the authority it has obtained has been received from the Papacy. By its authority, the Papacy has made Mary to appear like Christ Himself, and in Argentina in 1986, the apparition returned the favor. The vision of Mary reaffirmed the authority of the Papacy, saying that "priests must follow the pope for to walk by him is to walk by my Son Himself."[126] So while the Papacy transfers the attributes of Christ to Mary, the apparitions are transferring these same attributes back to the popes. Theirs is a very reciprocal relationship, and there is hardly an apparition occurring today that has not expressed these same sentiments.

In addition to these affirmations, several of the more notable apparitions, past and present, have actually requested that personal messages be relayed to the pope--sometimes privately, sometimes publicly. In Medjugorje in 1982, the apparition said the pope should "spread untiringly and with courage the message of peace and love among all mankind."[127] Private messages have also been given to the pope by the apparitions of Medjugorje,[128]

---

[125] *Signs of the Times Special Update #1*, distributed by *Signs of the Times Apostolate*, Sterling, Virginia, June 24, 1994, pg. 8. Message of November 15, 1951

[126] *Our Lady Queen of Peace*, "An Urgent Appeal: Our Lady in Argentina," pg. 7. Message of October 27, 1986. Used by permission.

[127] *Words From Heaven*, pg. 105. Message of September 26, 1982

[128] Graham, Anna, *Diary of a Pilgrim to Medjugorje*, December 4, 1988, pg. 8

LaSalette,[129] Fátima,[130] and others. The apparition of Mary, it seems, is quite grateful for the cooperation of the Papacy, and has encouraged popes at every turn to continue in their efforts. Their relationship is one of mutual admiration and of mutual benefit.

Of course this does nothing but establish that the apparitions and the Papacy have had an affectionate relationship with each other and that the Papacy, through the proclamation of the Marian doctrines, has provided the apparitions with exactly the justification they needed to appear as Mary in bodily form prior to the general resurrection. Which means that something masquerading as Mary has very effectively submitted to the authority of the Papacy and, more importantly, has used the authority bestowed on it--an authority that the Papacy was very sure it had bestowed on the mother of Jesus--to interact with visionaries. And through them, the apparitions are interacting with people everywhere. But one need only examine the teachings of the apparitions to determine that they are not the mother of Jesus at all. The Papacy by its doctrines has not only given the apparitions of Mary the authority they need in order to appear bodily, but has also given them the authority they need to preach salvation through the name of Mary--something, I contend, that the mother of Jesus would not do.

---

[129] Hasler, August Bernhard, *How the Pope Became Infallible: Pius IX and the Politics of Persuasion*, (New York: Doubleday & Company, Inc., ©1981) pp. 111-2

[130] Walsh, pg. 222-3

Authority to Deceive

Amen, amen, I say to you, no slave is greater than his master nor any messenger greater than the one who sent him.

--*John 13:16*

ESTABLISHING that the apparitions of Mary have received certain honors and even authority from the Papacy is one thing, but a discussion on the authority so-bestowed cannot end here. The obvious question is, Why was the transfer of authority necessary? It would make little sense for the apparitions to invest so much time and energy during the last twelve centuries only to make it doctrinally acceptable and logically possible for Mary to appear in bodily form. There must have been a motive. And while it is of interest to examine the transfer of messianic attributes from Jesus to Mary, it is even more important that we examine the actions that have followed upon the receipt of the authority. Indeed, what has the apparition of Mary done with what it has received from the Papacy? One need not look far to discover how the authority has been used.

Scriptures prove to us that Jesus suffered and died in our place. He is our Redeemer, our Mediator, our High Priest, our Messiah and our Advocate. If any of us should sin, we have a Redeemer Who suffered for us, a Mediator Who intercedes for us, and a High Priest Who offered Himself for us.

We have a Messiah Who saved us.

This is our assurance. This is our foundation. This is our Gospel, the Gospel of Jesus Christ. One would think that His mother, if she were so inclined, would come to teach us the truth about the Truth. One would expect that she would know the Gospel of her Son. One would think that she would know the Word of God.

And indeed, Mary most assuredly does. But whatever it is that has been masquerading as Mary for the last twelve centuries seems to be familiar with none of these. In fact, the apparitions of Mary have done nothing but breed confusion about who saved us, and by what means He did so.

Mary as Redemptress

Jesus Christ suffered for us in our place to pay for our sins. So teach the Scriptures:

> "...but we do see Jesus 'crowned with glory and honor' because he suffered death... that by the grace of God he might taste death for everyone."[131]

The scriptural argument is quite sound in and of itself. Who would deny that Jesus' sufferings are sufficient for the payment of our sins?* And who would desire that this truth be withheld from anyone? Yet the apparitions of Mary have done exactly that, for they have made Mary's sufferings equivalent to Jesus', and they have intentionally blurred the distinction between the two. The following quotes are by no means a complete list of such assertions by the apparitions, but they are, nonetheless, typical:

Apparition of Mary to Lucia Abóbora, Fátima, Portugal 1917

> "'Jesus ...wishes to establish in the world the devotion to My Immaculate Heart' ..[Lucia later recalled,] 'Before the palm of the right hand of Our Lady was a Heart encircled by thorns which seemed to have pierced it like nails. We understood

---

131 Hebrews 2:9

* It is a curious thing indeed that Paul's words in Colossians 1:24 are sometimes taken to mean that he too suffered in our place, for he says, "in my flesh I am filling up what is lacking in the afflictions of Christ on behalf of his body." However, the only times that Paul actually reveals what his sufferings are accomplishing (Philippians 1:12-18, 2 Timothy 2:8-10, etc.), he makes it clear that his sufferings always resulted in the *preaching* of the Gospel, which was in fact the only thing that was lacking at the cross.(Romans 10:14-15)

> that it was the Immaculate Heart of Mary outraged by the sins of humanity, for which there must be reparation.'"[132]

Apparition of Mary to Julia Kim, Naju, South Korea 1985-present

> "I pray without ceasing for those of my children who have fallen into vice and corruption, suffering in their place."[133]

Apparition of Mary to Nancy Fowler, Conyers, Georgia, USA 1987-present

> "Our Loving Mother said, 'We are both revealing our suffering faces to you. Tell others we suffer for them in love.'"[134]

> "During the vision, Jesus appeared to Nancy on the cross and, then, merged with an image of His Mother. This vision was repeated over and over and over and over. This vision appeared to show the oneness of their suffering."[135]

These messages are just a sampling of the many which teach along the same vein, and they all serve to make one thing clear: if anyone thought that the apparitions had in any way desired to make known the sufferings of Jesus and the redemption wrought for us by them we have here substantial evidence that the apparitions of Mary do not desire to teach this at all. By using such confusing imagery as Mary's heart surrounded by thorns and Mary merging with Jesus on the cross, the apparitions make it clear that they have not chosen, as Paul did, "to know nothing while I was with you except Jesus Christ, and *him* crucified."[136]

---

[132] Walsh, pp. 68-9. Brackets added for clarity

[133] "Marian Apparitions of the 20th Century: A Message of Urgency," a video narrated by Ricardo Montalban. Produced and written by Drew J. Mariani and Anne McGeehan-McGlone. Directed by Drew J. Mariani. Produced at the Eternal Word Television Network, Birmingham, AL. Marian Communications, Ltd., ©1991, International Copyrights Reserved

[134] *To Bear Witness*, pg. 99, para. 172. Message of February 2, 1991

[135] *To Bear Witness*, pg. 68, para. 86. Vision of March 29, 1991

[136] 1 Corinthians 2:2. Emphasis added

The apparitions have even gone so far as to assert that Mary suffers for us in our place for our sins. There is no clear reflection of the Gospel of Jesus Christ here, and there is no clear teaching on His sufferings and what they accomplished for us. The apparitions of Mary have, in fact, withheld the Gospel from those who follow them. And even though Bernadette Soubirous, the Lourdes visionary, described the apparition as "...a young and very beautiful lady,"[137] the visions have made it clear by their words that they are not the lowly handmaid that the Scriptures portray. In fact, the apparitions have lied both about their identity and about the Gospel of Jesus Christ.

Mary as Mediatrix

Jesus Christ is the Mediator between sinful man and a Holy, Righteous God. So teach the Scriptures:

> "For there is one God.
> There is also one mediator between God and the human race,
> Christ Jesus, himself..."[138]

The scriptural argument is quite sound in and of itself. Who would deny that Jesus is our only mediator? And who would desire that this truth be withheld from anyone? Yet the apparitions of Mary have done exactly that, for they have made Mary our mediator, and have for all practical purposes ignored the unique mediating role of Jesus Christ in their teachings:

Apparition of Mary to Pierina Gilli, Montichiari, Italy 1947

> "I have place(sic) myself as the mediatrix between my Divine Son and mankind, especially for the souls consecrated to God."[139]

---

[137] Cranston, Ruth, *The Miracle of Lourdes*, (New York: Doubleday & Company, Inc., ©1955, 1983, 1988) pg. 33

[138] 1 Timothy 2:5

[139] *Our Lady Queen of Peace*, "Mystical Rose: Mother of the Church," pg. 17. Message of October 22, 1947. Used by permission

Apparition of Mary to the children of Medjugorje, Bosnia 1981-present

"I am a Mediatress between you and God."[140]

Apparition of Mary to Therese Lopez, Denver, Colorado, USA 1991-present

"I ask you to pray and ask boldly from me. I will intercede in front of God for you."[141]

If anyone thought that the apparitions had in any way desired to make known that Jesus is the one Mediator between God and man, we have here substantial evidence that the apparitions of Mary do not desire to teach this at all. By using such confusing imagery as Mary holding back the wrath of her Son, or Mary interceding for us before God, the apparitions make it clear that they have not chosen, as Paul did, to make known that "we have boldness of speech and confidence of access through faith in him (Jesus Christ)."[142] There is no clear reflection of the Gospel of Jesus Christ in the teachings of the apparitions, and there is no clear exposition on His mediating role and the assurance believers now have because of it. The apparitions of Mary have, in fact, withheld the Gospel from those who follow them. And even though Therese Lopez, the Denver visionary, when explaining the appearance of the apparition said that "There are no words to describe the beauty of that face,"[143] the visions have made it clear by their words that they are not the lowly handmaid that the Scriptures portray. In fact, the apparitions have lied both about their identity and about the Gospel of Jesus Christ.

Mary as High Priestess

Jesus Christ is our High Priest Who offered Himself before God to redeem us from all unrighteousness. So teach the Scriptures:

---

[140] O'Carroll, pg. 181. Message of July 17, 1986
[141] Kuntz, pg. 43. Message of February 23, 1991
[142] Ephesians 3:12
[143] Kuntz, pg. 18

"It was fitting that we should have such a high priest: holy, innocent, undefiled, separated from sinners, higher than the heavens. He has no need, as did the high priests, to offer sacrifice day after day, first for his own sins and then for those of the people; he did that once for all when he offered himself."[144]

The scriptural argument is quite sound in and of itself. Who would deny that Jesus offered to God the only Sacrifice which could appease His wrath? And who would desire that this truth be withheld from anyone? Yet the apparitions of Mary have done exactly that, for they have made Mary our High Priest, and have for all practical purposes attempted to remove Jesus Christ from His proper function of offering the one redemptive Sacrifice on our behalf:

Apparition of Mary to Sister Mary of Agreda, Spain circa 1617

"Then She offered to the eternal Father the blood, which his Son shed in the Circumcision and his humility in allowing Himself to be circumcised in his sinlessness."[145]

Apparition of Mary to the children of Medjugorje, Bosnia 1981-present

"I am with you and day after day I offer your sacrifices and prayers to God for the salvation of the world."[146]

Apparition of Mary to Sister Agnes Sasagawa, Akita, Japan 1973-1981

"With my Son I have intervened so many times to appease the wrath of the Father. I have prevented the coming of calamities by offering Him the sufferings of the Son on the Cross, His

---

144 Hebrews 7:26-28

145 Mary of Agreda, *Mystical City of God*, Volume IV, *The Coronation*, pg. 565, para. 666

146 *Caritas of Birmingham,* "Messages From Our Lady," September-December 1990 issue, pg. 1. Message of November 25, 1990

> Precious Blood, and beloved souls who console Him forming a cohort of victim souls."[147]

If anyone thought that the apparitions had in any way desired to make known that Jesus is our worthy High Priest Who offered the Sacrifice for sins once and for all, we have here substantial evidence that the apparitions of Mary do not desire to make this clear at all. By using such confusing imagery as Mary offering the blood of Jesus to appease the anger of God, or Mary offering the sufferings of Jesus before God's throne, the apparitions make it clear that they have not chosen, as Paul did, to make known that "Jesus Christ... gave *himself* for us to deliver us from all lawlessness and to cleanse for *himself* a people as his own, eager to do what is good."[148] There is no clear reflection of the Gospel of Jesus Christ in the teachings of the apparitions, and there is no clear explanation of His High Priestly role and the fact that God's wrath is now completely satisfied because of it. The apparitions of Mary have, in fact, withheld the Gospel from those who follow them. And even though Vicka Ivankovic, one of the Medjugorje visionaries, explained that "Our Lady looked at us with a beautiful sweetness,"[149] the visions have made it clear by their words that they are not the lowly handmaid that the Scriptures portray. In fact, the apparitions have lied both about their identity and about the Gospel of Jesus Christ.

Mary as Savior

Jesus Christ is our Savior Who rescues those who place their trust in Him. So teach the Scriptures:

> "There is no salvation through anyone else, nor is there any other name under heaven given to the human race by which we are to be saved."[150]

---

[147] *Our Lady Queen of Peace*, "Church Approves Messages, Weeping Statue as Supernatural," pg. 16. Message of August 3, 1973. Used by permission

[148] Titus 2:13b-14. Emphasis added

[149] *Words From Heaven*, pg. 85

[150] Acts 4:12

The scriptural argument is quite sound in and of itself. Who would deny that Jesus is the Savior God sent into the world? And who would desire that this truth be withheld from anyone? Yet the apparitions of Mary have done exactly that, for they have made Mary our savior, and have not only attempted to share Christ's role in redemption, but have removed Him from that role altogether:

Apparition of Mary to Sister Agnes Sasagawa, Akita, Japan 1973-1981

> "I alone am able still to save you from the calamities which approach. Those who place their confidence in me will be saved."[151]

Apparition of Mary to the children of Medjugorje, Bosnia 1981-present

> "I seek your prayers, that you may offer them to me for those who are under Satan's influence, that they may be saved."[152]

Apparition of Mary to Julia Kim, Naju, South Korea 1985-present

> "I wish to save the world by the victory of my mercy and love. That is why my Immaculate Heart will triumph."[153]

If anyone thought that the apparitions had in any way desired to make known that Jesus is our Savior, we have here substantial evidence that the apparitions of Mary do not desire to make this clear at all. By using such confusing imagery as Mary saving us by her mercy and love, or Mary asking us to place our confidence in her, the apparitions make it clear that they have not chosen, as Paul did, to make known that it was Jesus Who "brought you to life along with him, having forgiven us all our transgressions."[154]

---

[151] *Our Lady Queen of Peace*, "Church Approves Messages, Weeping Statue as Supernatural," pg. 16. Message of October 13, 1973. Used by permission

[152] O'Carroll, pg. 222. Message of February 25, 1988

[153] "Marian Apparitions of the 20th Century: A Message of Urgency"

[154] Colossians 2:13b

There is no clear reflection of the Gospel of Jesus Christ in the teachings of the apparitions, and there is no clear expression of His role as Savior and the assurance we now have because of it. The apparitions of Mary have, in fact, withheld the Gospel from those who follow them. And even though Estela Ruiz, the Phoenix visionary, described the apparition as "the most beautiful lady I had ever seen,"[155] the visions have made it clear by their words that they are not the lowly handmaid that the Scriptures portray. In fact, the apparitions have lied both about their identity and about the Gospel of Jesus Christ.

Mary as Goddess

Jesus Christ is God, uniquely incarnate in human flesh, condescending to rescue us. So teach the Scriptures:

> "In the beginning was the Word,
> and the Word was with God,
> and the Word was God.
> ...And the Word became flesh
> and made his dwelling among us."[156]

The scriptural argument is quite sound in and of itself. Who would deny that Jesus is God Himself in the flesh? And who would desire that this honor be shared with anyone but God alone? Yet the apparitions of Mary have done exactly that, for they have made Mary a goddess in her own right, and by doing so have attempted to obtain for the apparitions the glory of which only Christ is worthy:

Apparition of Mary to the children of Medjugorje, Bosnia 1981-present

> "I ask you once more to pray especially for my intentions. If you pray for my intentions I will be glorified through you."[157]

---

[155] *Our Lady Queen of Peace*, "Our Lady of the Americas," pg. 8. Used by permission
[156] John 1:1, 14
[157] O'Carroll, pg. 259. Message of November 26, 1988

Interior Locution of Mary to Carlos Lopez, San Francisco, California, USA
1991-present

> "I am the Morning Star whom announces the day, the Light which is near, the Light of God, the Light of Love, the Light of peace, the Light of eternal salvation... I will ascend to heaven to take possession of My throne alongside of My Son."[158]

Apparition of Mary to Maximin Giraud and Melanie Mathieu, LaSalette, France
1846

> "I gave you six days for working. The seventh I have reserved for myself."[159]

If anyone thought that the apparitions had in any way desired to make known that Jesus Christ is God Almighty, we have here substantial evidence that the apparitions of Mary do not desire to make this clear at all. By using such confusing imagery as Mary ascending to her throne in Heaven, or being glorified through us, or having the seventh day of the week reserved to honor her, the apparitions make it clear that they have not chosen, as Paul did, to make known that only "in him dwells the whole fullness of the deity bodily."[160] There is no clear reflection of the Gospel of Jesus Christ in the teachings of the apparitions, and there is no clear confession of His position as the exalted, ascended God of all creation, and the assurance we now have because of His promise. The apparitions of Mary have, in fact, withheld the Gospel from those who follow them. And even though Maximin Giraud and Melanie Mathieu, the LaSalette visionaries, explained that the apparition had "the most beautiful face they had ever seen," and had a voice that "sounded like music,"[161] the visions

---

[158] *Signs of the Times*, Volume 6, Number 2, April/May/June 1994, "Heaven's Global Tapestry," pg. 49. Message of February 2, 1994. Compare this statement against Revelation 22:16

[159] Lord, *The Many Faces of Mary*, pg. 70. Message of September 19, 1846

[160] Colossians 2:9

[161] Lord, *The Many Faces of Mary*, pg. 69

have made it clear by their words that they are not the lowly handmaid that the Scriptures portray. In fact, the apparitions have lied both about their identity and about the Gospel of Jesus Christ.

And so it is that while the Papacy, believing the apparitions to be Mary, has done everything in its power to bestow on them the attributes of Jesus Christ, the apparitions have followed suit and have mirrored the intentions of the Papacy. The apparitions' teachings highlighted above are only a small sampling of the thousands of messages given by the apparitions. And all of them, to a greater or lesser degree depending on the specific apparition, have cooperated with the expressed intentions of the Papacy to portray Mary as a savior of mankind. The teachings of the apparitions, though scripturally unsound, merely reflect the doctrines that the Papacy has already put forth about Mary. In fact, the Fátima, LaSalette, and Agreda apparitions, all of which were cited above, have been officially approved at various levels within the Catholic Church. Even the messages from the Denver visions, also cited above, were dismissed by Archbishop Stafford as "devoid of any supernatural origin," yet were described by the Archdiocesan vicar general Raymond Brown as containing nothing "contrary to the faith."[162]

So while it is true that the apparitions have appeared to the many visionaries throughout history in the most disarmingly innocent manner one could possibly imagine--as the mother of Jesus--it is also true that they have taught a gospel that is completely incompatible with their claims to be Mary. It is likewise true that the Catholic Church has found nothing particularly offensive about the apparitions' statements. More importantly, the teachings of the apparitions merely reflect the claims that the Papacy had been making about Mary all along.

Suffice it to say that the apparitions, while appearing to be rather harmless and peaceful to the many visionaries, are teaching a deadly gospel which is not as harmless as they would have us believe. Deceptive, dangerous and unnervingly beautiful is what the apparitions of Mary are. And by using the authority bestowed on them along with the appearance of beauty, the apparitions have

---

[162] *Signs of the Times*, Volume 6, Number 2, April/May/June 1994 edition, "Marian News Update: Denver Archbishop Releases Statement --Lopez Group Responds," pp. 6-7

insured that no one will suspect what their teachings make clear: that they are not at all whom they claim to be. The apparitions of Mary, while appearing peaceful and harmless, have taught a doctrine of falsehood and have done so by the authority given to them by the Papacy.

Visual Confirmation

> The signs of an apostle were performed among you with all endurance, signs and wonders, and mighty deeds.
>
> --*2 Corinthians 12:12*

FOR Catholics, perhaps it is sufficient that the apparitions of Mary teach Roman Catholic doctrines and affirm the authority of the Papacy. If these teachings do not gain more Catholic followers for the apparitions, at the very least they limit opposition within the ranks. Some Catholics, though remaining unconvinced of the spiritual manifestations, are satisfied to let the apparitions' followers show excitement about visions as long as they do not stray from Catholic truth. And though the apparitions have yet to maximize their harvest of souls within the Catholic Church, they have at least acknowledged that their efforts beyond the bounds of Catholicism will require more than just an affirmation of papal primacy. Protestants, not surprisingly, do not find such affirmations convincing. They need more than that, and the visions of Mary have been happy to provide it. Having successfully demonstrated their ability to convince a predominantly Catholic audience, the apparitions of Mary have turned to something more persuasive to the non-Catholic seeker: miracles. If an interested Protestant seeker wished to find some semblance of the miraculous in the apparitions of Mary, the visions have more than satisfied this desire.

A July 20, 1987 *Newsweek* article reported that the apparition at Medjugorje, Bosnia, had been performing signs and wonders for its followers. Among the most notable signs were, the Croatian word for peace, 'MIR,' written across the sky, "mysterious fires, columns of light," and other visions including the appearance of Christ's face on the cross.[163]

Ann Marie Hancock, in her book *Be A Light: Miracles at Medjugorje*, also reported such phenomena as rosary chains miraculously turning to gold, a burning bush that was not consumed, the appearance of bright lights with no apparent source flooding the village, and perhaps most notably, a 15 ton concrete cross that spun so fast as to appear as a pillar of light.[164]

Similar miraculous signs had occurred at Fátima many years earlier. Monsignor Joao Quaresm, an eyewitness to the apparitions there, wrote that he had the opportunity to see Mary descending from the heavens in a globe of light.[165] At the Shrine of Lourdes, location of the 1858 apparitions, miracles are still being performed as well, including many which involve documented cases of people being cured of terminal illnesses.[166]

Pilgrims and visionaries in Betania, Venezuela, a current apparition site (and location of one current bleeding host phenomenon), have also experienced unexplainable miraculous events. The video production, "Betania: Land of Grace," a documentary on the Betania apparitions, informs us:

> "People have testified seeing a mysterious fog that seems to come out from the trees and the hill, intense light that would brighten the hill, and at times a profusion of flowers that would cover it, especially roses. Sounds of hymns from an invisible choir are often heard. Still others have reported strange lights and movements in the sun. The water from the cascade at times acquires the perfume of roses, while others claim to have received mysterious rose petals from [the] heavens..."[167]

These miracles are but a few of the many that have been performed at the hundreds of apparition sites around the world,

---

163 *Newsweek*, July 20, 1987, Volume 110, "Visitations of the Virgin," pg. 55

164 Hancock, Ann Marie, *Be A Light: Miracles at Medjugorje*, (Norfolk/Virginia Beach, Virginia: The Donning Company Publishers, ©1988) pp. 58-61

165 Walsh, pg. 126-7,200-1

166 Cranston, pg. 261

167 "Betania: Land of Grace." Brackets added for clarity

and they vary from site to site. Other miracles have included such prodigies as the Medjugorje apparition actually summoning a woman from the dead at the request of the woman's daughter;[168] the Bayside, New York apparition predicting the April 1993 bombing of the World Trade Center;[169] and the Akita, Japan apparition causing statues to weep human tears or tears of blood.[170] There are many, many more miracles and wonders being performed by apparitions even now, and they are no doubt accomplishing what they expected: to convince both Catholics and Protestants alike that the visions are truly from God.

As one might expect, Catholics have been very responsive to the miracles, and Ted and Maureen Flynn, both lifelong members of the Catholic Church, give evidence of this. Maureen Flynn, who co-authored the recently popular pro-apparition book *The Thunder of Justice* with her husband, Ted, testifies to the fact that her conversion to Mary can be traced back to a miracle she saw while on pilgrimage to Medjugorje.[171] Michael H. Brown, also a lifelong Catholic and former secular journalist, is the author of *The Final Hour*, a book about modern Marian apparitions. He testifies that his conversion to Mary began with a miraculous vision of Michael the Archangel giving him instructions on how to ward off evil,[172] and another vision of a blue "globule of light" with the face of Mary in it.[173]

The Protestant response has been similar, as some of the most vocal proponents of the current apparitions of Mary are former Protestants who converted to Roman Catholicism because of

---

168 Hancock, pg. 40

169 Information on this specific prophecy can be found in two newsletters of the Bayside apparition dated October 1, 1988, and April 7, 1993. The newsletter is entitled *Roses*, and can be obtained from Our Lady of the Roses Shrine, PO Box 52, Bayside, New York, 11361-0052.

170 "Marian Apparitions of the 20th Century: A Message of Urgency"

171 *The Atlanta Journal-Constitution*, Sunday, June 12, 1994, "Apparition followers see warning in recent events," pp. A1, A8

172 *Signs of the Times*, Volume 5, Number 2, March/April 1993, "Michael Brown Speaks On Spiritual Warfare And Catholic Action," pp. 25-6

173 Brown, Michael, in his speech, *The Final Hour: An Urgent Message*, recorded and distributed by The Mary Foundation

these miracles. Among them are Wayne Weible, former Lutheran and author of such books as *Letters From Medjugorje* and *Medjugorje: The Message*; and Scott Hahn, former Presbyterian minister and co-author of *Rome Sweet Home*, a book about his journey from Protestantism to the Catholic faith. Wayne Weible testifies that his conversion to Mary began when he attended a Sunday School class on modern day miracles.[174] Scott Hahn testifies that his conversion to Catholicism was deeply affected by the resolution of a "seemingly impossible situation" after fervent prayers to Mary through the Rosary, and that he has since "fallen head over heels in love with our Lord in the Eucharist!"[175] Have the miracles of the apparitions been successful in harvesting Protestant souls? They surely have.

And though I find it unfortunate that so many Protestants have joined the ranks of those who submit to the pope, follow the apparitions and worship the Eucharist, I will do no more than acknowledge the obvious: the apparitions have been performing many, many signs and wonders and have been accomplishing their apparent desire to gain a following. Protestant conversions aside, this phenomenon can be summarized by saying that the apparitions of Mary, by the authority received from Rome, have taught a false gospel and at the same time have performed many miracles to convince people of their authenticity. That said, I will move on to what is considered among the followers of the apparitions to be the most convincing sign of all.

---

174 Weible, Wayne, *Miracle at Medjugorje: A series of columns on a modern-day supernatural religious event,* "You are my son…" pg. 1, from an article published in December of 1985

175 Hahn, Scott and Kimberly, *Rome Sweet Home: Our Journey to Catholicism*, (San Francisco, CA: Ignatius Press, ©1993) pp. 68, 88

The Fire of Heaven

And suddenly there came from the sky a noise like a strong driving wind... Then there appeared to them tongues as of fire, which parted and came to rest on each one of them.

--Acts 2:2-3

IN addition to the many signs, wonders and miracles that occur at every apparition site, there is one unique, repeating miracle that links almost every such site in the world. It is called the Miracle of the Sun, the Phenomenon of the Sun, or the Dance of the Sun. At Fátima, on October 13, 1917, there were 70,000 people present to witness it.[176] It happened again before a crowd of 100,000 in Puerto Rico on April 23, 1991, which was the 38th anniversary of the apparitions there,[177] and it happened once again in the Philippines on March 5, 1993, in front of a crowd of 300,000.[178] Similar events have been recorded at such apparition sites as Medjugorje, Bosnia; Denver, Colorado; Lubbock, Texas; and Conyers, Georgia.

The first recorded incident of the Dance of the Sun was also the most spectacular. At one of the apparition's first visits in Fátima, Portugal in 1917, the child visionary Lucia Abóbora inquired of it, "What is it you want of me?" The apparition replied that on the thirteenth of each month Lucia should return to the same location to recite the rosary. The apparition promised that at

---

[176] Walsh, pp. 145-50

[177] *Our Lady Queen of Peace*, "Our Lady of the Rosary in Puerto Rico," pg. 13

[178] *The Tennesseean*, Volume 89, Number 66, March 7, 1993, "Filipinos flock to glimpse vision of Mary," pg. 2A

the final visit, it would "perform a miracle so that all shall believe."

The last month finally came, and 70,000 eyewitnesses experienced an event of apocalyptic significance. They saw the sun directly overhead and of normal brightness, yet they were able to look directly into it without blinking. It began to spin and "dance," which is the origin of the term 'Dance of the Sun.' While 'dancing,' it began flinging blood-red light in every direction, followed by pulsations of light from all colors of the spectrum, each color in proper succession. "Madly gyrating in this manner three times, the fiery orb seemed to tremble, to shudder, and then to plunge precipitately, in a mighty zigzag, toward the crowd... This lasted about ten minutes," after which time the sun resumed its normal position and brightness in the noon sky over Portugal. Far from being a case of mass hysteria, eyewitnesses as distant as 18 kilometers away described the miracle, saying that the sun, "...seemed to come down in a zigzag, threatening to fall on the earth."[179] William Thomas Walsh, in his book, *Our Lady of Fátima*, summarized the miracle, saying,

> "As early as May, 1917, Jacinta and Lucia had told people that the Lady they saw had promised a miracle on October 13, at the hour of noon, as a sign of their sincerity... On the very day and hour they had foretold, some 70,000 persons testified that they had the unique experience of seeing the sun spin round and seem to fall."[180]

This has not been an isolated event. The same phenomenon has been recorded at the Medjugorje apparition site, with very similar eyewitness descriptions. All who observe the phenomenon seem to experience the vivid color changes and the appearance of the sun first getting closer, then further away. Ann Marie Hancock was an eyewitness to such an occurrence at Medjugorje, and she writes,

> "The sun appeared to be spinning on its own axis. It also seemed to move toward the observers and then recede. A great darkness loomed behind the sun as the sun moved toward the crowd. ...I found myself staring at this vortex of gold,

---

179 Walsh, pp. 120,145-50

180 Walsh, pp. 145-50

> seemingly covered by a disc that protected my eyes. ...As it spun, it seemed to move towards us... The colors were vibrant fuschia, violet, lavender, silver, and emerald."[181]

Bob and Penny Lord, both enthusiastic proponents of the apparition phenomenon, also experienced the miracle when they visited Medjugorje on June 28, 1985:

> "At the time when Our Lady was to appear, everybody ran to the left of the rectory to look at the sun, poised in the sky, between the church and the rectory. I wasn't about to follow them, but some of the children from our group called me over. There was an urgency in their voices. I ran over to where the crowd was, and looked up at the sun. Though it was a clear day without clouds, I could look right into the sun without being blinded by its brightness. It moved; it danced; it whirled. It shot out bolts of various colors, blue, green, and yellow. It seemed to become larger. Then it stopped. It moved back to its original position. It became too bright to look into it, as it had been before the movement had begun."[182]

The same events have been recorded at Sabana Grande, Puerto Rico, which experienced apparitions in 1953. On May 25th of that year, the apparition treated the spectators to the Phenomenon of the Sun. Then on the 38th anniversary of the first Sabana Grande apparition, the vision was repeated:

> "On April 23, 1991, with over 100,000 people present, the Miracle of the Sun and other solar phenomena were reported at Sabana Grande."[183]

In Lubbock, Texas, USA, a location which has recently experienced visitations of the apparition of Mary, many pilgrims have experienced the same Dance of the Sun:

> "On August 15, 1988--The Feast of Our Lady's Assumption into Heaven--an estimated 20,000 people assembled on the

---

[181] Hancock, pp. 61-62

[182] Lord, *The Many Faces of Mary*, pg. 200

[183] *Our Lady Queen of Peace*, "Our Lady of the Rosary in Puerto Rico," pg. 13

grounds of St. John Neumann Church in Lubbock, Texas. It had been announced that there would be a sign on this day... Many people say they saw the sun 'dance.'"[184]

In Agoo, Philippines, also known for its Marian apparitions, the sun has been known to go through the same cycle, as well. On March 5, 1993, in front of a crowd of 300,000 people, the Miracle of the Sun was seen:

> "Others claimed to see the sun turn color and dance in the sky. Many in the crowd wept and chanted prayers as the hours past(sic). 'I saw the sun coming out in different colors,' cried a nearly hysterical Ching Dario, who had come from Manila. 'It was first coming down, then it went up again.'"[185]

In Denver, Colorado, USA, at the Mother Cabrini shrine, Josyp Terelya was also given the opportunity to see this Dance of the Sun. Terelya is a traveling locutionist and is a very active proponent of the apparitions and their messages. After visiting the site of the Denver apparitions in October of 1991, he related his experience to an audience of 7,000 in Chicago, Illinois:

> "I saw the miracle of the sun and the sun spinning. I started to pray. My whole body, my whole body trembled with such a joy I cannot explain it to you. I knelt down, and as I knelt, I heard a voice say, 'Josyp, within a year's time, here in this place, very many miracles will take place. It will be a very great pilgrimage center just like Fatima and Medjugorje.'"[186]

In a slight deviation from the norm, the apparition of Mary at El Cajas, Ecuador, added a new twist to the Miracle of the Sun by causing 'sun drops' to fall on the many pilgrims at the scene of the apparition:

> "Mary appeared there [in El Cajas] with golden skin and 12 stars--calling herself 'Guardian of the Faith.' Crowds of up to

---

184 *Our Lady Queen of Peace*, "Apparitions: Lubbock, Texas (1988)," pg. 9

185 *The Tennesseean*, Volume 89, Number 66, March 7, 1993, "Filipinos flock to glimpse vision of Mary," pg. 2A

186 Kuntz, pg. 19

> 120,000 ascended the heights, like a scene out of *Exodus*. During the ecstasies lights like golden raindrops fell from the sun..."[187]

There are innumerable other eyewitness accounts of this miracle, and they all testify to events similar to those witnessed by the 70,000 at Fátima in 1917. They all report seeing the sun move or vibrate in the sky, turn to all the different colors of the spectrum, and then either plummet toward the crowd and return to the sky, or at the very least, appear to move closer and then farther away. No apparition site has ever experienced the dramatic solar plummet that the pilgrims of Fátima did (i.e., the sun dropping from the sky and then 'hovering' over the crowd for 10 minutes), but the effects are the same. Because of the strange and profoundly impossible nature of the miracle, many have come to believe that the apparitions of Mary are exactly whom they claim to be.

I do not wish at this point to argue about whether or not it is theologically correct for the apparitions of Mary to make the sun come down to earth while hundreds of thousands of people are looking on. Neither do I wish to argue about the astrophysical implications of the miracle. Instead, I wish only to establish that the apparitions have indeed performed these miracles. That much we can verify based on the eyewitness accounts. Consistently and increasingly, the apparitions of Mary have been making the sun appear as if it was coming down from heaven to earth in the sight of everyone. Astrophysical impossibilities notwithstanding, the apparitions have done this. The eyewitnesses all testify to it.

What hundreds of thousands, and even millions of people have seen at Fátima, Medjugorje, Lubbock, Denver, Conyers, Sabana Grande and Agoo is nothing less than the remarkable ability of the apparitions to make the sun come down to earth as crowds of people stand by and observe with awe. But one cannot grasp the sheer magnitude of the number of people who have seen this without first considering the size of the crowds who travel as pilgrims to each apparition site (See Table 1, following page).

When one considers that the data in Table 1 are just the attendance statistics for *one day*, (and several of these apparition

---

[187] Brown, Michael H., *The Final Hour*, (Milford, OH: Faith Publishing Company, ©1992) pg. 315. Brackets added for clarity, italics in original

sites are now celebrating 40-, 80-, 100- and 450-year anniversaries), the number of pilgrims who are witnessing the miracle of the sun *yearly* is astounding. This great number does not even include the people who visit *between* the anniversary events. For example, from 1981 to 1989, there were more than 15 million pilgrims to the Medjugorje apparition site alone,[188] and that was well before Medjugorje ascended to the media prominence it now enjoys as a major site of Marian apparitions.

Popular Apparition Sites	Anniversary attendance
Fátima	1,000,000+
Lourdes	250,000+
Guadalupe	3,000,000+
Conyers	100,000+
Sabana Grande	100,000+

Table 1: Attendance at apparition sites on anniversaries and other significant dates[189]

Though it is true that not all pilgrims see the Miracle of the Sun, it is difficult to argue with the millions of eyewitnesses who have. I do not wish to contend with them. Suffice it to say that literally millions and millions of people visit apparitions sites yearly, and a great many of them not only see a good number of miracles, but they also tend to see the most interesting one of all: the sun coming down to earth and going back up again. It can be said with great accuracy, then, that the apparitions of Mary have, by the authority received from Rome, taught a false gospel and have performed many miracles to convince people of their authenticity, even to make fire come down from heaven to earth as people look on.

---

188 "Medjugorje: The Lasting Sign," a video narrated by Martin Sheen. Directed by Rob Wallace. Produced by Cinematic Visions, Inc., ©1989, All Rights Reserved

189 Guadalupe, Fátima and Lourdes references from Lord, *The Many Faces of Mary*, pg. 23. Conyers reference is from the *Journal of Reported Teachings and Messages of Our Lord and Our Loving Mother at Conyers, Georgia, USA*, dated November 1993, pg. 1, and the Sabana Grande reference is from *Our Lady Queen of Peace*, Special Edition I, dated Winter 1992, pg. 13

Part 3: Handmade

'Cursed be the man who makes a carved or molten idol--an abomination to the LORD, the product of a craftsman's hands--and sets it up in secret!' And all the people shall answer, 'Amen!'

--Deuteronomy 27:15

A Mark of Distinction

> ...they issued a decree to be proclaimed throughout all Israel from Beer-sheba to Dan, that everyone should come to Jerusalem to celebrate the Passover in honor of the LORD, the God of Israel; for not many had kept it in the manner prescribed.
>
> --*2 Chronicles 30:5*

REMEMBRANCE and obedience. These two terms sum up the purpose and meaning of the Communion celebration. "Do this in memory of me."[190] The love behind the action Jesus was about to perform on the Cross demands that we remember. His Person demands that we obey. This Jesus Who broke bread and poured wine for His disciples that day in 30 AD is the same God Who instructed Moses with nearly the same words almost 1500 years earlier:

> "For seven days you shall eat unleavened bread, and the seventh day shall also be a festival to the LORD. Only unleavened bread may be eaten during the seven days... On this day you shall explain to your son, 'This is because of what the LORD did for me when I came out of Egypt.' ...Therefore, you shall keep this prescribed rite at its appointed time from year to year."[191]

In effect, God was instructing Moses to "Do this as a remembrance of Me," just as Jesus would one day tell His apostles. To Moses, the Passover was a reminder of what God had

---

[190] Luke 22:19b
[191] Exodus 13:6-8,10

done for the Hebrews. To us, the Passover Supper is a reminder of what God accomplished for us in His Son's death. The same fear that drove Moses to obey exactly as instructed also drives us to obey Christ's words exactly as He spoke them.

But what did Jesus say? In His own words,

> "While they were eating, Jesus took bread, said the blessing, broke it, and giving it to his disciples said, 'Take and eat; this is my body.' Then he took a cup, gave thanks, and gave it to them, saying, 'Drink from it, all of you, for this is my blood of the covenant, which will be shed on behalf of many for the forgiveness of sins.'"[192]

Jesus said the bread was His body. I will not argue about literal interpretations, but I know what He did not say. Jesus *did not* say of the bread, "This is My blood." He merely took it and said it was His body. Likewise, Jesus *did not* say of the wine, "This is My body." He merely passed the cup and said it was His blood. That is all He said.

Likewise, when Jesus presided over the Last Supper, He did not administer the bread by itself as if that was the completion of the rite of Communion. Neither did He add water to the wine and serve it to His apostles as a diluted mixture. Rather, He administered first the bread and then the undiluted wine and commanded: "Do this." *Exactly this.* That is why in Christian congregations today, when communion is celebrated, the bread is passed first, and then the wine. Because that is what Jesus taught us to do.

Though it is clear from the Bible what Jesus did and did not say, it is important to establish precisely what transpired when He partook of His Last Supper, because our obedience to His command requires that we understand what He did that day. And according to Jesus' instructions, the Lord's Supper is not complete without either of the two elements--or species--of bread and wine. Communion exists as both bread and wine, or it does not exist at all. That is how Jesus instituted it, and that is how He wanted to be remembered. And when God speaks, His people obey. That is our mark of distinction.

---

192 Matthew 26:26-28

And precise obedience is important when it comes to the mandates of a perfect God. That is not to say that there is no room for human error, and nobody knows like God does how difficult it is for us to obey perfectly. But while God has in this matter of the Passover been merciful where human error is manifested,[193] He has rarely shown patience for outright and willful disobedience. Jesus commanded unconditionally, "Do this." So we do. Any corruption of His command, or any omission from His instructions, represents a willful divergence from a ritual that God Himself ordained.

So how shall we respond if someone instructs us to partake only of the bread of communion without the wine, assuring us that the bread is sufficient in itself as a fulfillment of Christ's command? What if someone instructs us to mix water with our wine when we celebrate this meal, assuring us that Christ would likely give His blessing? Would such actions suffice? Would they fulfill the commands of Christ? Would our actions then be actions of obedience? Or would they be actions of willful disobedience?

In our modern world where ecumenism is the order of the day, we must consider such questions, and we must turn to the Bible to find our answers. If we are instructed to partake of Communion in a manner that Christ did not intend and in a way that He did not institute, we must know what we believe, and we must know why we believe it. I will not argue about whether or not the bread and wine literally become the body and blood of Jesus, because that is not the issue of this book. I will not expound on the finer points of transubstantiation, consubstantiation, or the like. But I will assert that when Jesus commands us to remember Him, we ought to obey by remembering Him in the way He wished to be remembered. Simple, Biblical obedience to the command of a perfect God--that is all I am suggesting.

The Bible may tell me that the bread is Jesus' body, and that the wine is His blood, but this is *not* what the Catholic Church teaches. The Church of Rome states that the bread not only becomes the body of Jesus, but that it becomes His blood as well. That being the case, it is considered proper to receive the Sacrament of Communion under only one of the two species, i.e., in the form of bread alone. It is held by the Catholic Church that

---

193 2 Chronicles 30:14-20

receiving communion under the form of bread alone is sufficient as a fulfillment of Jesus' command. But that is not what the Bible says. That is not what Jesus taught us, and it is not how He asked to be remembered.

The Council of Trent stated that the body and blood of Jesus were both fully present in each form of the Communion elements, the bread and wine, even when separated. According to the Catholic Church, receiving Communion in the form of bread alone is therefore considered sufficient because the bread is purported to contain both the body *and* the blood of Jesus. But this was taken one step further. Receiving Communion under the form of bread alone became mandatory, and the Cup was officially withheld from Christians who wanted to partake of both species. The 1917 *Code of Canon Law* makes this clear, as Canon 852 reads:

> "The most holy Eucharist is to be distributed under the species of bread alone."[194]

Why? Because the bread is purported to contain both the body and the blood of Jesus, so the blood of Jesus, strictly speaking, is not truly withheld from the believer--it only appears that way. The 1994 *Catechism of the Catholic Church* reaffirms this teaching, stating,

> "Since Christ is sacramentally present under each of the species, communion under the species of bread alone makes it possible to receive all the fruit of Eucharistic grace."[195]

In other words, willful disobedience to the command of Christ is of no consequence. The doctrine which asserts that the blood of Jesus is present in the form of bread makes administration of the wine unnecessary. Bob and Penny Lord, advocates of the apparitions of Mary and of Eucharistic worship, are not doctrinal experts, but they make clear what the implications of this teaching are. In their recent book, *This is My Body, This is my Blood: Book*

---

[194] Neuner, Josef, S. J. & Roos, Heinrich, S.F., *The Teaching of the Catholic Church*, (New York: The Mercier Press, ©1967) pg. 301

[195] *The Catechism of the Catholic Church*, Part 2, Section 2, Chapter 1, Article 3.VI, "The Paschal Banquet," paragraph 1390

II, they refer to the teachings of the Catholic Church regarding this practice:

> "Although the Host *appears* to represent solely the Body of Jesus, it has always been *completely* the *Body and Blood* of Our Lord Jesus... Therefore, when we receive the Host, we are receiving the complete Jesus, in His Body, Blood, Soul and Divinity... At this point in the Mass, Mother Church is demonstrating *definitively* this truth that has come down through the ages that when we receive under either one of the Holy Species, we are receiving *fully* the Lord in His Body, Blood, Soul and Divinity."[196]

I do not here use Bob and Penny Lord to prove doctrine, but rather to demonstrate application. On the authority of the Catholic Church, the Lords have dispensed with Christ's command to "Drink from it, all of you,"[197] and have accepted a substitution. The doctrine indeed leads to the willful disobedience of Jesus' commands at the Last Supper. And though some Catholic churches today administer the Sacrament of Communion under both species, the authority of the Church has taught as recently as the Second Vatican Council that administration of bread alone is mandatory except in special cases "when the bishops think fit."[198] And the Roman Catholic Church still teaches today that bread alone suffices as the memorial meal. To assert the contrary was considered un-Christian at the Council of Trent:

> "If anyone shall deny that in the venerable sacrament of the Eucharist the whole Christ is contained under each form and under every part of each form when separated--*anathema sit*."[199]

> "If anyone shall deny that Christ ...is received whole and entire under the one species of bread, because, as some falsely

---

[196] Lord, *This is My Body, This is My Blood: Miracles of the Eucharist, Book II*, pp. 307-8. Emphases in original

[197] Matthew 26:27b

[198] *The Teachings of the Second Vatican Council*, Section 1, Chapter II, "Of the Mystery of the Holy Eucharist," paragraph 55 (Westminster, MD: The Newman Press, ©1966)

[199] The General Council of Trent, Session XIII (1551): DS 1653

> assert, he is not received in accordance with the institution of Christ under both species--*anathema sit.*"[200]

Anathema sit. 'Let him be accursed.' If anyone should dare to deny that it is sufficient to receive the Sacrament of Communion in the form of bread alone, he has separated himself from the Body of Christ and receives a *de facto* excommunication from the Church. The teaching of the Catholic Church has been very clear on this point.

But again, I return to the two main emphases of the command of Christ: remembrance and obedience. Jesus said that we should partake of the Communion meal first in the bread, then in the wine. Obedience to Him demands that we partake of both. Not one or the other, but both.

Receiving both species represents obedience to Christ. The Scriptures teach exactly that. Receiving only one of the species represents obedience to the Catholic Church. The Council of Trent taught exactly that.

So the issue is a matter of choosing between two authoritative mandates. Jesus said, "Take and eat... Drink from it, all of you."[201] The Papacy says, "Take and eat, but do not drink." Obedience to one demands willful disobedience to the other.

And this issue extends beyond that of taking Communion solely in the form of bread, because even though the Catholic Church occasionally allows lay people to receive the Cup, it is still required that the wine first be mixed with water. I will not argue about what kind of wine Jesus used during the Supper, but I do know that Jesus offered the fruit of the vine to His apostles. Just fruit of the vine, not wine mixed with water. Obedience to His command requires that we partake of Communion with bread and wine, obeying without question, not turning to the right or to the left. Yet the Catholic Church has not only taught that it is proper to mix water in the wine of communion, but has gone so far as to teach that it is mandatory. Anything else is considered un-Christian. The Council of Trent stated it this way:

> "The Holy Council then calls to mind that the Church has instructed priests to mix water with the wine that is to be

---

[200] The General Council of Trent, Session XXI (1562): DS 1733

[201] Matthew 26:26-27

> offered in the chalice, because it is believed that Christ the Lord did so, and also because from his side there came blood and water; the memory of this mystery is renewed by this mixture..."[202]

> "If anyone shall say ...that water ought not to be mixed with the wine that is to be offered in the chalice because it is contrary to the institution of Christ--*anathema sit*."[203]

Anathema sit. 'Let him be accursed.' If anyone should deny that it is proper to mix water with the wine of communion, he has separated himself from the Body of Christ and has received a *de facto* excommunication from the Church.

Again, the issue in the celebration of Communion is that of obedience. Jesus said that we should partake of Communion using wine. Not wine mixed with water. And though it is a laudable desire to call to mind that both water and blood came forth from Jesus' side, mixing water with wine is not how Christ wanted to be remembered.

Using undiluted wine during the Lord's Supper represents obedience to Christ. The Scriptures teach exactly that. Mixing water with wine during Communion represents obedience to the Catholic Church. The Council of Trent taught exactly that.

So the issue at hand is a matter of choosing between two authoritative mandates. Jesus said, "Drink from it, all of you."[204] The Papacy says, "Do not share the cup among yourselves. But if you do, dilute the wine with water first." Obedience to one demands willful disobedience to the other.

This is not to criticize anyone for his choice, but only to establish that the choice has been made. I have willfully disobeyed the clear teaching of the Council of Trent by insisting that the Communion meal be taken under the form of bread and wine together. I have willfully disobeyed the clear teachings of the Council of Trent by insisting that the wine of communion not be mixed with water as a part of the meal.

Likewise, the Council of Trent has willfully disobeyed the clear teaching of Scripture by prescribing the Communion

---

[202] The General Council of Trent, Session XXII (1562): DS 1748

[203] The General Council of Trent, Session XXII (1562): DS 1759

[204] Matthew 26:27

celebration in a different manner than Jesus instituted it, and so have those who partake of communion according to the instructions of the Council of Trent. The Council of Trent has willfully disobeyed the clear teaching of Scripture by mixing with water what Jesus served undiluted, and so have those who partake of communion according to the instructions of the Council of Trent. If the Council felt it had the authority to refine the institution of Christ, then so be it. I did not write this to question its authority, but merely to establish that following its teachings requires a choice between what Jesus taught us in the Bible and what the Council taught us in the mid-1500s. A choice has been given, and a choice has been made.

Why do I emphasize this point? Because the central theme of the celebration of Communion is *obedience* to Christ's command: "Do this." And obedience is the distinguishing mark of the people of God. This is not without precedent. In Ezekiel 9, God commands that a mark be placed on the foreheads of all "who moan and groan over all the abominations that are practiced."[205] Those who obeyed God had His mark placed on their foreheads. Those who did not were slaughtered. Another example is found in Revelation 14:1, where the 144,000 have God's name and the Lamb's name written on their foreheads. Their distinction? They had obeyed. They were "the servants of our God."[206]

Likewise, when God instituted the rite of the Passover meal--a ritual involving unleavened bread and which is the predecessor of the New Testament Communion meal--He said that obedience to His mandate would be an indication that we had accepted Him as our authority. He instructed Moses that participation in the Passover meal was a way that the Jews would receive a distinguishing mark of obedience to God:

> "For seven days you shall eat unleavened bread, and the seventh day shall also be a festival to the LORD. ...On this day you shall explain to your son, 'This is because of what the LORD did for me when I came out of Egypt.' It shall be as a sign on your hand and as a reminder on your forehead."[207]

---

205 Ezekiel 9:4b

206 Revelation 7:3

207 Exodus 13:6, 8-9

Participating in a ritual of unleavened bread is 'as a sign' on the hand and 'as a reminder' on the forehead. Moses' use of the word 'sign' here is the same word that he used in Genesis 4:15, "So the LORD put a *mark* on Cain."[*] According to God's own Word, participation in the Passover ritual is the same as receiving a distinct mark on the hand and on the forehead. Likewise, when Christians partake of the Passover Supper, the Supper instituted by Jesus Christ and mandated by His Father, we receive a mark on our forehead and on our hands as a reminder of what God did for us at Calvary. According to what God teaches us in His Word, any time Christians obey Him by following His commands, and particularly when we partake of the Lord's Passover Supper, we receive a mark of distinction on our hands and foreheads. But the mark is conferred only when we obey Him *exactly* as He instructed. Notice in the following Scripture that the mark of obedience to God, and the subsequent fruits of obedience, are conditioned upon *exact* compliance:

> "Therefore take these words of mine into your heart and soul. Bind them at your wrist as a sign, and let them be as a pendant on your forehead. ...For if you are careful to observe all these commandments I enjoin on you, loving the LORD, your God, and following His ways *exactly*, and holding fast to him, the LORD will drive all these nations out of your way..."[208]

His mandate is for us to follow His commands *exactly*.[†] By doing so, we receive on our hands and forehead a mark of

---

[*] Emphasis added

[208] Deuteronomy 11:18,22-23. Emphasis added

[†] This is not to propose in any way that we are somehow *justified* by our obedience to Christ. Rather, it is to emphasize what Paul so clearly taught in Romans 1:5, in order "to bring about the obedience of faith, for the sake of his name..." The unbiblical liturgy of the Catholic Church would not be such a hurdle were it not for the fact that the Council of Trent condemned people to hell for refusing to practice the illicit rituals of diluting the wine and withholding the Cup. Because of Christ, we are called to obey. The Catholic Church tells us otherwise. Its wrongful instruction that we should willfully violate what Christ instituted cannot go without a biblical challenge to obey the higher authority, especially in

continued on next page

distinction that makes us His. Likewise, when Catholics follow the mandates of the Council of Trent regarding the celebration of the Passover Supper, the Eucharist, they too receive a mark of distinction--a mark which indicates their obedience to the Council of Trent and to the hierarchy of the Catholic Church. As I stated earlier, a choice must be made between celebrating Communion as Christ instituted it, and celebrating it as the Council of Trent described it; it is not possible to satisfy both Christ's instructions and those of Trent. A choice must be made between the two, and a choice has been made.

I do not wish to criticize Catholics for their obedience to the Council of Trent, but wish rather to establish that when anyone participates in the Passover Supper, the Communion meal instituted by Christ, he receives a mark of distinction on his hands and forehead--a mark that indicates to whom he has pledged his obedience.

And when Catholics adore the Communion bread, worship it publicly or carry it in procession for the purpose of venerating it in accordance with the instructions of the Council of Trent, they receive a mark indicating their obedience to the popes who have instructed throughout history that the Eucharist is to be worshipped. And when they partake of Communion in the form of bread alone, or with diluted wine, they accept a mark of distinction which indicates their obedience to the Papacy.

This is not mere conjecture. It is exactly what God has said about the breaking of the Passover bread. It is exactly what the pre-Incarnate Jesus Christ told Moses when He gave him instructions on how to celebrate the Passover, and it is exactly what Jesus Christ confirmed when He said, "Do this in remembrance of me." This institution of Christ, whether we ever knew it or not, places a mark on our hands and foreheads *according to God's own design.* Whether Protestant or Catholic, a mark is given. To Christians who celebrate according to the Bible, a mark of obedience to Scripture. To Catholics who celebrate according to the Council of Trent, a mark of obedience to the Papacy.

---

light of the fact that Rome instructs us to worship the very ritual that has so diverged from the clear instruction of Christ.

In His Image

> They spoke of the God of Israel as though he were one of the gods of the other peoples of the earth, a work of human hands.
>
> --*2 Chronicles 32:19*

IT is no difficult task to demonstrate that the Papacy has instructed people to worship the bread of the altar, the Eucharist. Neither is it difficult to prove that the apparitions have encouraged the same. In all of this the Church Councils, the popes, and the apparitions have concurred emphatically throughout history: the bread of the altar is to be worshipped, given the same reverence that is due to the Almighty God, Yahweh, the God of Israel. Knowledgeable Catholics are quite aware of this, Church Councils have mandated it, and the apparitions' many followers have gone to great lengths to establish the practice as widely as possible. And history demonstrates what the Papacy and the apparitions have been encouraging all along--the bread of the altar has been worshipped for centuries. And it has been worshipped at the instructions of the popes and the apparitions of Mary.

What is also proven by mere inspection, not to mention the documentation of the Catholic Church, is that the Eucharist is made by human hands. Though the bread of the altar is purported to be changed into the body and blood of Jesus Christ, the appearance of bread which remains is still the result of the efforts of the hands of men. It is indeed merely the work of a human. This is established from the Order of the Sacrifice of the Mass, a step-by-step procedure for the Rite of the Eucharist. When the priest offers to God the sacrifice of the altar, he does so first by thanking Him for providing the elements of bread and wine for the sacrifice:

"Blessed are you, Lord, God of all creation. Through your goodness we have this bread to offer, which earth has given and human hands have made. It will become for us the bread of life."[209]

Transubstantiation or the True Physical Presence of Jesus aside, the Order of the Mass begins with an outright confession that the bread which is about to be worshipped is bread that 'human hands have made.'* This is not to ignore the belief in actual Transubstantiation, and neither is it to forget the good intentions of those who worship the bread believing it to be God. Rather, it is to establish first that the Mass contains a clear confession that the focus of the ensuing worship is an item which is handmade.

Likewise, the order of the Mass also includes a prayer of which even the Catholic Church confesses no knowledge of origins. When the priest has consecrated the bread and wine, believing it to become the Body, Blood, Soul and Divinity of Jesus Christ, he makes use of a prayer called the *Secreta*, or literally, "The Prayer Said in Secret." In his book, *This is the Mass*, written under the instruction of Archbishop Fulton J. Sheen, Henri Daniel-Rops wonders out loud, as it were, about what the *Secreta* really means:

"Why is it called *Secreta*? ...does this name indicate that we here have a prayer of introduction to the *secret things*, to the

---

[209] *Sunday Missal Prayerbook and Hymnal for 1994*, "Liturgy of the Eucharist: Preparation of the Gifts," (NY: Catholic Book Publishing Company, ©1993) pg. 20

* Invariably the Roman response to this is that the bread becomes Jesus Christ Who cannot be an image of Himself, and Who is most certainly *not* made by human hands. However the natural antecedent to any discussion on Transubstantiation is the question of whether a New Testament priestly class was ever established by Jesus Christ. If there is no separate New Testament class of priests, then there is no power to transubstantiate the bread and wine. If there is no New Testament priestly class, then the bread remains bread, and therefore remains "what human hands have made." Robert M. Zins, Th.M., deals with this quite well in his chapters on the Eucharist and the Mass in *Romanism: The Relentless Roman Catholic Assault on the Gospel of Jesus Christ,* (Huntsville, AL: White Horse Publications, ©1995) pp. 111-129

> King's mysteries? Whatever be the historical origin of the term, it is now generally translated as *the prayer said in secret.* For it is most quietly that the celebrant enunciates these words..."[210](all italics original)

'Whatever be the historical origin of the term.' Quite a statement considering that the Mass is purported to be an exact reenactment of the Last Supper. But whether or not the prayer said in secret has legitimate historical origins, it is certainly part of the Mass now and has been for centuries, and the use of this prayer which the priest utters 'most quietly' was affirmed by the Council of Trent. According to the Council, failing to utter the prayer said in secret 'most quietly' was considered un-Christian:

> "Holy Mother Church has instituted certain rites, namely that some things in the Mass be pronounced in a low tone and others in a louder tone... If anyone shall say that the rite of the Roman Church whereby a part of the canon and the words of consecration are pronounced in a low tone is to be condemned... *anathema sit.*"[211]

Anathema sit. 'Let him be accursed.' If anyone dare to deny that the celebration of the Lord's Supper should necessarily include a part that is performed 'in secret,' or 'in a low tone,' he has separated himself from the Body of Christ and has received a *de facto* excommunication from the Church. This curse applies to anyone who suggests that, because Christ mentioned no such thing when He instituted the Lord's Supper, "the prayer said in secret" should not be part of the Lord's Supper.

This is not to ignore the good intentions of those who publicly worship the bread believing it to be God, but rather to establish first that the Mass contains a segment which is done 'in secret,' the *Secreta,* and that the Council of Trent steadfastly affirmed the practice. The 1994 *Catechism of the Catholic Church* takes this one step further and suggests that an effective means of worshipping the consecrated bread is to retire to a Church building and worship the bread there, 'in secret':

---

210 Daniel-Rops, Henri, *This is the Mass*, as celebrated by Archbishop Fulton J. Sheen, (New York: Hawthorn Books, Inc., ©1958) pg. 84

211 The General Council of Trent, Session XXII (1562): DS 1746, 1759

"The church, the house of God, is the proper place for the liturgical prayer of the parish community. It is also the privileged place for adoration of the real presence of Christ in the Blessed Sacrament... For personal prayer, this can be a 'prayer corner' with the Sacred Scriptures and icons, in order to be there, in secret, before our Father."[212]

And though in making this statement the 1994 *Catechism* calls to mind Jesus' mandate in Matthew 6:6 to pray in a private location, it must be clarified that the *Catechism* instructs people to do this in the presence of icons and with the intention of worshipping the Eucharist, whereas Jesus only mentioned this in terms of humble prayer to the Father. This is not to criticize those who, in addition to the many forms of public worship of the bread, opt also to worship the bread in secret. Rather, it is to establish that worshipping the bread in secret is in perfect conformity with the teachings and instructions of the Catholic Church. After first publicly declaring during the Mass that the bread is indeed made by human hands, the Catholic Church then instructs the faithful to worship the bread in secret. Whether some feel this is right or wrong does not change the fact that this is indeed what the Catholic Church teaches. It is of interest then that there are several Biblical mandates which absolutely prohibit such worship as this. These prohibitions are,

1) we are not to make or worship an image of God,
2) we are not to worship what is made by human hands, and
3) we are not to erect in secret and worship an object which is handmade.

Directly from Scripture, we read these prohibitions:

"You saw no form at all on the day the LORD spoke to you at Horeb from the midst of the fire. Be strictly on your guard, therefore, not to degrade yourselves by fashioning an idol to represent any figure..."[213]

---

212 *The Catechism of the Catholic Church*, Part 4, Section 1, Chapter 2, Article 3, "Guides For Prayer," paragraph 2691
213 Deuteronomy 4:15

> "You shall not carve idols for yourselves in the shape of anything in the sky above or on the earth below or in the waters beneath the earth."[214]

> "Cursed be the man who makes a carved or molten idol--an abomination to the LORD, the product of a craftsman's hands --and sets it up in secret!"[215]

The Scriptures make clear to us that we shall not worship a handmade image (even if it is a handmade image of the True God), and we certainly are not to erect it in a secret place for adoration. Such behavior is strictly prohibited and falls into one singularly offensive category: idolatry. Regardless of whatever historical justification the Catholic Church may provide for a defense of the practice, the Scriptures state authoritatively that Eucharistic Worship is nothing short of image worship and idolatry.

It is indeed interesting that a faithful Catholic will not only affirm the above Biblical prohibitions emphatically, but also at the same time and with equal emphasis, will affirm the practice of worshipping, in secret, or in public, the Eucharist which 'human hands have made.' Worshipping in secret that which is made by human hands is not only a standard part of the Liturgy of the Eucharist, the Mass, but is also central to the Catholic faith. This conclusion is not drawn by mere conjecture, but rather directly from the official documents and rituals which outline the faith of the Catholic Church. And it is significant that when the charges of worshipping in secret what is made by hand are leveled against a knowledgeable practicing Catholic, instead of being met with denial, the charges are met with an enthusiastic admission: 'Yes! We *do*!' And in doing so, faithful Catholics, whether knowingly or not, receive a mark of distinction which indicates their practice of worshipping in secret what is made with human hands--a mark which is given when they worship an image, the idol of the Eucharist--and that they have done so at the insistence of the Papacy and the apparitions of Mary.

---

[214] Deuteronomy 5:8

[215] Deuteronomy 27:15

The Wonders of Technology

...nor is he served by human hands because he needs anything.

--*Acts 17:25a*

SOUNDS like nuclear war to me!" Such was the exposition my friend provided for Zechariah 14:12. The plague in that verse is graphically described as rotting skin, rotting eyes, and rotting tongues in the mouths of the unfortunates who were afflicted with it. Was it possible that Zechariah had foretold the development of such advanced weaponry in this verse, weaponry that could literally melt the skin off of the human body? No such technology could have existed in Zechariah's day! What an accurate prophecy of nuclear war! Sometimes this is assumed without question. I have heard Sunday School lectures in which Zechariah 14:12 was confidently exposited as evidence that the Great Tribulation of Matthew 24 would involve nuclear weapons. Hal Lindsay himself is a major proponent of such an interpretation. He writes,

> "The nature of the forces which the Lord will unleash on that day against the armies gathered in the Middle East is described in Zechariah 14:12... A frightening picture, isn't it? Has it occurred to you that this is exactly what happens to those who are in a thermonuclear blast? It appears that this will be the case at the return of Christ."[216]

---

216 Lindsey, Hal with Carlson, C. C., *The Late Great Planet Earth*, (Grand Rapids, MI: Zondervan Publishing House, ©1970) pg. 175

And in light of recent history, in light of the damage inflicted by the United States of America on Nagasaki and Hiroshima during World War II, it is difficult to interpret that passage any other way. Unless, of course, one looks back further than 1945.

It was in 1096 that the call went forth from Rome to the people of Europe: We must "wrest away from 'The wicked race' the Holy Sepulchre" and take Jerusalem back from them.[217] Though many popes had for years attempted to accomplish that very thing, no one was so successful as Pope Urban II at the Council at Clermont. After his impassioned speech that worked the crowd into a frenzy, the famous cry was heard, a cry which would resound throughout Europe and the Mediterranean nations for the next 150 years: "God wills it! God wills it!"[218] The Crusades had begun.

Millions of people traveled on foot, horseback, ponyback or by ship to Jerusalem--often from such remote regions as Norway and Sweden, but more commonly from England and the contiguous nations of what eventually became modern Europe. For 150 years, European Catholics arrived at the gates of Jerusalem to fight for its capture, scale its walls and to return it to its rightful owner--the Catholic Church. During those years, the Crusaders endured the most trying circumstances: slavery, hunger, thirst, imprisonment, and torture. But nothing claimed so many lives as the hideous disease that they contracted when they arrived in Israel.

Zoé Oldenbourg, in her book, *The Crusades*, details the symptoms of the debilitating affliction which the Crusaders endured upon their arrival in the Holy Land:

> "Their bodies remained in the gully dividing the two camps and for weeks the smell of decomposition made the air unbreathable, while clouds of flies bred new diseases. In the full heat of August and lacking proper food, the soldiers had little resistance to disease and the death rate was terrible. The constant arrival of forces compensated for the losses, but the newly landed men also fell victims to disease in their turn. Philip, Count of Flanders, died a few days after his arrival at Acre, and Philip Augustus and Richard Coeur-de-Lion also

---

[217] Flick, Alexander Clarence, Ph.D., Litt.D., *The Rise of the Mediaeval Church*, (New York: The Knickerbocker Press, ©1909) pp. 488-9

[218] Flick, pg. 489

> nearly died in the holy war before they had a chance to do any fighting. Both in turn were ravaged by a strange disease which made the skin fall from their bodies, and they almost lost their sight. The two Kings were young, strong, and well cared for and they recovered; there is no knowing how many soldiers died."[219]

Malcolm Billings, in his work, *The Cross and the Crescent*, reports this 'strange disease' as well:

> "Many lives and horses were lost but disease was the Christians' greatest enemy, according to James of Vitry. It was, 'a contagious disease with no natural causes, divinely sent down on a great part of our army either to cleanse us from our sins or so that we should be more deserving of the crown. For the thighs and legs first swelled up and then festered; also superfluous flesh grew in the mouth.' Between one fifth and one sixth of the army were said to have died in the epidemic... 'The sickness that had stricken the army now began to increase to such an alarming extent, and so many people suffered from mortification of the gums, that the barber surgeons had to remove the gangrenous flesh before they could either chew their food or swallow it. It was pitiful to hear around the camp the cries of those whose dead flesh was being cut away; it was just like the cry of a woman in labour.'"[220]

'Strange disease,' indeed. Their skin literally rotted on their bodies, they lost their vision, and they grew 'superfluous flesh' in their mouths. Rotting skin, rotting tongues, eyes rotting in their sockets. Such an uncomfortable disease, and for what crime? They had come to fight against Jerusalem.

There was no exchange of nuclear weapons between the Crusaders and the Jewish and Muslim occupants of the Holy City. There was no advanced technology that could cause such symptoms. Only a simple plague with no known natural causes. Just a plague, and just what God had prophesied when He caused Zechariah to write:

---

219 Oldenbourg, Zoé, *The Crusades*, (NY: Random House, ©1966) pg. 452

220 Billings, Malcolm, *The Cross and the Crescent*, (NY: Sterling Publishing Co., Inc., ©1987) pp. 145, 163

> "And this shall be the plague with which the LORD shall strike all the nations that have fought against Jerusalem: their flesh shall rot while they stand upon their feet, and their eyes shall rot in their sockets, and their tongues shall rot in their mouths."

Whether or not one believes that the Crusaders' disease was the fulfillment of Zechariah's prophecy, it becomes clear that nuclear weapons were not needed to fulfill it. And while nuclear weapons can certainly cause the symptoms described by Zechariah, God has a great many means of wrath at His disposal and does not need our technology to accomplish His will. He is infinite, and He is infinitely powerful. Our technology does not aid Him and neither does it hinder Him. And He certainly has never had to stoop to our level of technology to accomplish His purposes. This chapter is not about the Crusades against Jerusalem, but this information will help me to make my next point, because it seems that we have acted with a similar--and unwarranted--technological mind-set in our exposition of other Bible verses as well.

When we read such prophecies as that of Revelation 13:16, about the Mark of the Beast, we often do so with a certain bias toward our own level of technology. It would be impossible, we reason, to accomplish what the Beast of Revelation accomplishes unless he had at his disposal an awesome technology that John could not have understood when he prophesied it. Consider a recent exposition of that verse by a noted eschatologist:

> "We do not know how the mark will be imprinted on the hand or the forehead. Given modern technology, however, there are numerous ways this could be accomplished. A tiny microchip, for example, could be imbedded just under the skin in the palm of the hand. ...it seems unlikely that the mark would be a series of numbers crudely branded on the hand or forehead, but it will be a mark nonetheless that clearly identifies the man with either the name of the beast or the number of his (Antichrist's) name."[221]

---

221 Van Kampen, Robert, *The Sign*, (Wheaton, IL: Crossway Books, ©1992) pg. 223. Parentheses in original

Such was the exposition that Robert Van Kampen provided for Revelation 13:16 in his 1992 book, *The Sign.* This interpretation is not uncommon and neither is the notion that we are the first generation capable of fulfilling the prophecy of Revelation 13. This exposition was supported by Peter Lalonde in his immensely popular video, "The Mark of the Beast." In the introduction to that video he states,

> "The prophecy of the mark of the Beast is ...important because it pinpoints as a pure matter of fact that we are the first generation with the technology available to fulfill such a prophecy."[222]

Bar codes, Universal Product Code (UPC) symbols, credit cards, and microchips can all be used to facilitate financial transactions and all could be the predecessor of the technology used in a cashless society. Laser scanners to read our credit cards and orbiting satellites to track our movements. And we have developed them just in time. The technology that God needs to fulfill His prophecies of Revelation is now ready for Him to use, and the events are about to unfold. Or are they?

Such interpretations as these necessarily require a *subjective* approach. *We* are the first generation to develop the technology, and therefore *we* are the first generation capable of understanding the prophecy. But that is truly the height of arrogance. This is not to suggest that our interpretations of Scripture should exclude an assessment of the signs of the times, for even Jesus taught that we should be constantly aware of current events.* I do not reject a study of current events as long as it does not preclude an investigation into the Word of God. Yet I fear that this is exactly what has happened in our interpretation of the Mark of the Beast.

In Revelation 13 though 20, God reveals to us that the antichrist will require people to accept a mark on the forehead and on the hand, and will force people to worship an image of their own making. Our attention, therefore, should not be focused on our technology, but rather on what God reveals to us in His Word

---

222 Lalonde, Peter, "The Mark of the Beast," produced by Peter Lalonde and Tim Deibler, An Omega-Letter Video Production, ©1992, all rights reserved

* Luke 12:56

about a mark on the forehead and hand. As it turns out, there are only three references in Scripture, aside from the Mark of the Beast, to activities which result in a mark on one's hand and on one's forehead. They are:

The study of the Word of God	Deuteronomy 6:6-8
The consecration of the first-born	Exodus 13:15-16
The use of the Passover bread	Exodus 13:7-9

These are the only three references God makes in Scripture to activities that necessarily result in a mark on the forehead and on the hand. And more importantly, of these three, only one of them involves the use of something that is made by human hands: the Passover bread. The study of the Word results in a mark given because of something God wrote. The consecration of the first-born results in a mark because of a symbolic ritual that God ordained. But the celebration of the Passover necessarily involves the use of something that human hands have made: bread.

So when we read in Revelation 13:14-16 that the Beast will require people to worship an image of their own making and to accept a mark on their hands and forehead, our attention should first be drawn to the Scriptures to determine if there is anything in God's Word which involves both a mark on the forehead or hand and the use of something made by human hands. And when we discover that God has revealed to us in His Law that the Passover bread meets both of these requirements (and in fact is the only thing that does), our first course of action should be to find out if anyone is asking us, or forcing us, to worship the Passover bread, and to determine if anyone has caused that bread to come to life and possess the power of speech. It should not surprise us then that the image the Papacy has erected with the assistance of the apparitions of Mary is not just bread, but *Communion* bread which originates in the Passover ritual--bread which the Papacy has told us is really worthy of worship, and which God says results in a mark on the hand and forehead, bread which has for centuries been coming to life in Eucharistic miracles and at the same time has been speaking to those in adoration.

As I stated before, God has never needed to stoop to our level of technology to fulfill His prophecies. In fact, the 'technology' required to imprint a mark on the forehead and hand of the inhabitants of the earth has existed for millennia--a technology of

God's own design--and He has been using it quite effectively since its development. It was He, and not mere men, Who first asserted that participation in a ritual involving unleavened bread was the same as receiving a mark on one's hand or on one's forehead. It was He, and not mere men, Who first asserted that obedience to His command to remember Him during the Passover ritual was a means of receiving that mark of distinction.

So if one participates in the Catholic Church's unleavened bread ritual and worships the Eucharist, one receives a mark on the hand and on the forehead. This mark is not written there because of man's ingenuity, but because God so ordained it. And if anyone should question whether or not the mark received during an unleavened bread ritual is distinct enough to make it possible for a dictator to monitor the behavior of the population at large, we need only examine the testimony of the victims of the Inquisition. It is there that we find that the mark of worshipping the bread of the altar was distinct enough to strike fear into the heart of those who refused to adore it. It was distinct enough to make even the most outspoken keep their opinions to themselves, because they knew the consequences well:

> "By the end of the thirteenth century, ...its [the Inquisition's] arm was notoriously long, so that the very name already struck terror into every wavering heart."[223]

> "Even the kings of Spain themselves, ...were taught to dread the power of the lords of the Inquisition; and the horrid cruelties they exercised compelled multitudes, who differed in opinion from the Roman Catholics, carefully to conceal their sentiments..."[224]

The mark was as distinct as it needed to be. The Inquisitions were not only thoroughly effective in monitoring those who refused to receive the mark, but thoroughly terrifying to those who accepted it. How was it possible that the Inquisitors could be so effective without the aid of technology to track their unsuspecting victims from orbiting satellites? How could the Tribunals possibly monitor the conduct of literally millions of

---

223 Roth, pg. 37. Brackets added for clarity

224 Fox, pg. 60

people, and do so without the aid of modern computers? The answer is simple: they used methods that struck fear into the hearts of everyone. But more importantly, they used a 'technology' that was ordained by God, and not designed by man.

God did not need our assistance in developing a technology that was capable of imprinting a mark of distinction on the inhabitants of the earth in order to cause His prophecy to be fulfilled. All He needed was the feast of Passover, a ritual of unleavened bread that causes the participant to receive a mark of distinction on his hand or on his forehead. And that is what He ordained when He instituted the Last Supper as a remembrance of His Son, our Passover.[*] And that is what the Catholic Church fulfilled when it forced the inhabitants of the earth to worship the bread of the altar, bread which has come to life and has the power of speech.

---

* 1 Corinthians 5:7

The Power of Three

> It wielded all the authority of the first beast in its sight and made the earth and its inhabitants worship the first beast, ...telling them to make an image...
>
> --*Revelation 13:12,14b*

IT is a curiosity to me that when John recorded the Revelation of Jesus Christ, he equated image worship with accepting a mark on the forehead or on the hand. In Revelation 14:9-10, John explained that the wrath of God would be poured out on "Anyone who worships the beast or its image, or accepts its mark on forehead or hand." One verse later, he repeats that same equation, stating that the smoke of torment will forever rise "for those who worship the beast or its image or accept the mark of its name." In Revelation 16:2, festering boils are inflicted "on those who had the mark of the beast or worshipped its image." Again in chapter 19, verse 20, the pattern is repeated as John informs us that Jesus will one day destroy the beast and the false prophet who "led astray those who had accepted the mark of the beast and those who had worshipped its image." Finally, in Revelation 20:4, we are informed that the elect who reign with Christ will only be they "who had not worshipped the beast or its image nor had accepted its mark on their foreheads or hands."

In short, John uses the phrases "worship its image" and "accept its mark" almost as if one necessarily implied the other. It is interesting that John's tendency to link the two actually suggests that worshipping the image is the same as receiving a mark on one's hand or forehead. And this is only curious because the apparitions of Mary, by the authority of the Papacy, have for centuries encouraged the people of the world to worship a piece of bread--bread which, because of God's Passover ritual, is the same as receiving a mark on one's hand and forehead. The apparitions of Mary have instructed the people of the world to worship an image, the worship of which is the equivalent of accepting a mark. They could have instructed people to worship anything else in the world, yet they chose to instruct them to worship something that is, by definition, the equivalent of receiving a mark. And not just any mark, but a mark on one's hand and forehead.

I also find curious what John wrote in Revelation 13:14. I am no expert in Biblical languages, but the use of the word 'image' in that verse is interesting. Though I disagree with the majority of what Robert Van Kampen asserts in his book, *The Sign*, he does make a statement that caught my eye, and is worth mentioning here. Concerning the image of Revelation 13, he writes,

> "Dr. Robert Gundry, a noted New Testament and Greek scholar, ...confirmed my position that the Greek text could be interpreted either of ...two ways. In fact, his own position for some years has been that multiple images of the beast will be made and that everybody will be commanded to worship these images that will be set up for worship in various localities. He went on to say that the Greek term translated 'image' in this text can be taken (and here is best taken) as a collective singular, like our English words *crowd* or *people*. That collective noun could therefore represent a great number of separate images."[225]

In short, the reference to 'image' in Revelation 13, 14, 16, 19 and 20 could very possibly refer to one image which is replicated thousands--even millions--of times over and erected for worship in 'various localities.' This interpretation is particularly interesting considering that Pope John Paul II's recent statement to the 45th Eucharistic Congress about worldwide Eucharistic Adoration was exactly to that effect:

> "I hope that the fruit of this Congress results in the establishment of Perpetual Eucharistic Adoration in all parishes and Christian Communities throughout the world."[226]

---

[225] Van Kampen, pg. 476n. Parentheses and italics in original

[226] Pope John Paul II, June 1993, Seville, Spain. Address to the 45th Eucharistic Congress. *Signs of the Times*, Volume 6, Number 2,

continued on next page

Consider the implications of John Paul II's statement. Consider the implications of erecting an image for perpetual worship in every Christian community in the world. Now consider the fact that this very image was erected for public worship in many 'various localities' during the Inquisitions. And consider that this image has been set up for worship all over the world and is a means by which people receive a mark on their hands and foreheads. And consider that this image has been brought to life and has been given the power of speech.

But the similarities that the Papacy, the apparitions of Mary and the Eucharist share with the descriptions in Revelation 13 are myriad and are not limited just to the use of a particular image or a particular mark. The similarities go well beyond that.

Revelation 13 addresses three critical issues: that of the First Beast, that of the Second Beast (or False Prophet), and that of the Image. There are a great many details here, and I shall address them one by one. But according to this chapter in Revelation, the Beast, the False Prophet and the Image are visibly united in an effort to deceive an unsuspecting world. In obedience to the dragon, the threesome leads the world astray by imposing idolatrous worship of the Image of the First Beast. In a cooperative effort, the Beast first gives authority to the False Prophet, who then gives life and the power of speech to the Image, causing the inhabitants of the world to bow down and worship it. The Image, of course, is in honor of the First Beast, and the chain of honor and authority comes full circle. Does this sound familiar? It should.

The Papacy has for centuries bestowed honor and its own authority on the apparitions of Mary, calling them the Mother of God, the Immaculate Conception, and the Assumption--even the Queen of Heaven and Earth. With this authority, the apparitions of Mary began to demand that their followers spend time adoring the Eucharist, worshipping what is made with human hands. The image came to life, bleeding to prove that it was real, pulsating to show that it was alive, with the sole purpose of honoring the papal doctrines on the True Physical Presence of Christ in the Eucharist. The image spoke to the followers of the Papacy and encouraged them to continue in this practice, performing miracles to prove it

---

April/May/June 1994 edition, "Perpetual Adoration of the Holy Eucharist," pp.10-11

was supernatural. During the Inquisitions, the holy ones of God, who refused to worship the idol, were mercilessly tortured and slain when they chose to honor God above a piece of bread. Their finances were confiscated, their families and livelihoods taken away, and they were brutally beaten and tortured to death for refusing to worship the Eucharist. All of this because they would not worship a piece of bread which has its origins in the Passover--a ritual which by God's own design places a mark on the participant's hand and forehead.

And all of this was performed with the assistance of the apparitions of Mary. When the people of the earth doubted the authenticity of the visions, the apparitions began to perform a great many miracles, even making the sun appear to come down from heaven to earth in the sight of everyone. The apparitions have done this repeatedly in front of hundreds of thousands of people since Fátima in 1917, so that while appearing peaceful and harmless like a lamb, they could preach a false gospel like a dragon to the people of the world and have them believe. For more than one thousand years, this threesome--the Papacy, the apparitions of Mary and the Eucharist--have worked together to mislead millions. And they have been successful.

But this unity of three--the Beast, the False Prophet and the Image--is not new; in fact, it has been lurking at the horizon of Christianity for centuries. The Papacy has for hundreds of years enjoyed a comfortable, even affectionate relationship with the apparitions of Mary, and for as many years, the apparitions have encouraged the worship of the Eucharist. Together, these three have conspired to mislead the people of the world, and they rarely make mention of one without also mentioning the other. For example, Don Bosco, a canonized Roman Catholic saint and himself a Marian visionary, received a revelation in 1862 which detailed the criteria by which the Catholic Church would enjoy final victory over the earth. For reasons which will soon become obvious, the famous painting which depicts the elements of Bosco's vision can usually be found in any book that deals with devotion to Mary and the apparitions of the Virgin. In his vision, Bosco claimed to see this future cooperation between the Papacy, the apparitions and the Eucharist, because,

> "...it was revealed to him that peace in the world would come only after a fierce battle in which the Pope would triumph by

anchoring Peter's barque, the Church, to the secure pillars of the Eucharist and a fervent true devotion to Mary."[227]

It is worth noting that 'fervent devotion to Mary' has rarely in Roman Catholic history been known to prosper apart from the apparitions of Mary, in which case the pattern in Bosco's dream becomes rather interesting. Victory could only be obtained if the three were properly honored in unity: the Pope, the apparitions of Mary, and the Eucharist. The Beast, the False Prophet, and the Image. The power of three.

Therese Lopez of Denver Colorado has been receiving messages from the apparitions of Mary since 1991. When Therese was asked to summarize the basic teachings of 'Mary,' she explained that the apparition had three major requests:

> "*One*, to spread devotion and the consecration to her Immaculate Heart; *two*, to have fidelity to our Holy Father [the Pope]; and *three*, to maintain great reverence for Jesus' substantial presence in the Holy Eucharist. It is when these three things are kept in our foremost focus are we indeed responding to her message. ...We must strive to become the perfect imitation of her, ...support him [the Pope] as the head of the Holy Church, [and] ...spend time in Adoration before the Blessed Sacrament."[228]

Notice the pattern. Our obedience will be determined by honoring the three in unity: The Pope, the apparitions of Mary, and the Eucharist. The Beast, the False Prophet, and the Image. The power of three.

In his Sixth Encyclical, *Redemptoris Mater*, Pope John Paul II explained that Christians should be known for their devotion to Mary and their adoration of the Eucharist:

> "The piety of the Christian people has always very rightly sensed a profound link between devotion to the Blessed

---

[227] Flynn, Ted and Maureen, *The Thunder of Justice*, (Sterling, VA: MaxKol Communications, Inc., ©1993), verso of the half title page

[228] *Our Lady's Angels*, the official newsletter of the Conversion of Russia Prayer Group, St. Thomas More Center, Denver, Colorado, September 11, 1993, "How do I respond to Our Lady's Call," by Therese Lopez, pg. 3. Emphases in original, brackets added for clarity

> Virgin and worship of the Eucharist: this is a fact that can be seen ...in the traditions of the Religious Families, in the modern movements of spirituality, including those for youth, and in the pastoral practice of the Marian Shrines. Mary guides the faithful to the Eucharist."[229]

This Mary of whom John Paul II speaks, however, is not the Mary of the Bible, but rather is the Mary of the apparitions which claim to be her, as his many pilgrimages to apparition sites and his references to Marian Shrines clearly indicate. Notice then, the repeated pattern. Pope John Paul II teaches that as true Christians we ought to obey him and his predecessors by honoring the apparitions of Mary and worshipping the Eucharist. The Pope, the apparitions of Mary, and the Eucharist. The Beast, the False Prophet, and the Image. The power of three.

The famous apparition of Mary at Medjugorje has repeatedly honored the Papacy and encouraged John Paul II to continue in his work: "I wish to entrust to the Pope the word with which I came here: 'MIR' (peace), which he must spread everywhere."[230] But the apparition at Medjugorje also recommends that people worship the bread and wine of the Eucharist: "Unceasingly adore the Most Blessed Sacrament of the Altar."[231]

Notice the pattern. The apparitions of Mary encourage worship of the Eucharist and fidelity to the pope. The Pope, the apparitions of Mary, and the Eucharist. The Beast, the False Prophet, and the Image. The power of three.

In a special 'Eucharistic Edition' of *Signs of the Times,* a magazine dedicated to the propagation of the messages of the apparitions of Mary, an article appeared under the title "Our Lady of the Most Blessed Sacrament." In that article, the following statement was written:

> "The inseparable bond that exists between Mary and the Eucharist is brought out in several ways. One would be hard

---

229 Pope John Paul II, his Sixth Encyclical Letter *Redemptoris Mater*, (*Mother of the Redeemer*), Part III, Section 2: "Mary in the life of the Church and of every Christian," paragraph 44, March 25, 1987

230 *Words From Heaven*, pg. 273. Message of September 16, 1983. Parentheses in original

231 *Words From Heaven*, pg. 162. Message of March 15, 1984

> pressed to find a single Pope who would, at the same time, be dedicated to our Lady and have little or no devotion to the Eucharist, and vice versa. Mary and the Eucharist are intricately linked in the mind of the highest authority of the Church, the Papacy."[232]

The sole purpose of *Signs of the Times*, however, as noted above, is to disseminate the messages of Marian apparitions. In that case, then, the papal dedication 'to our Lady' is more accurately described as dedication to the apparitions of Mary. Notice the pattern that surfaces from their observation. The popes, the apparitions of Mary, and the Eucharist are intricately linked in a circle of devotion and worship. The Pope, the apparitions of Mary, and the Eucharist. The Beast, the False Prophet, and the Image. The power of three.

Youth 2000, a Catholic organization which sponsors youth weekends for Eucharistic Adoration, has a list of seven goals for the future in their statement of purpose. Among the "Aims of *Youth 2000*" are these:

> "To promote a true devotion to Jesus in the Holy Eucharist, creating a worldwide network of youth in prayer around the Blessed Sacrament.
>
> To promote a true devotion to Mary, the Virgin Mother of God, especially through the Rosary.
>
> To enable, encourage and embolden young people to respond to the Holy Father's [the Pope's] call to the Decade of Evangelization."[233]

But when *Youth 2000* refers to devotion to Mary 'especially through the Rosary,' they refer to a means of prayer which was given to the Church by the apparition of Mary to St. Dominic in 1206,[234] and revived by an apparition of Mary through Alan de la

---

[232] *Signs of the Times*, Volume 6, Number 2, April/May/June 1994, "Our Lady of the Most Blessed Sacrament," pp. 25-27

[233] *The Mir Response*, Volume 5, No. 4, August/September 1993 edition, pp. 8-9, 21, "Falling in Love ...With Jesus," by Mimi Kelly. Brackets added

[234] Ball, Ann, *A Litany of Mary*, (Huntington, IN: Our Sunday Visitor Publishing Division, Our Sunday Visitor, Inc., ©1988) pp. 117-20

Roche in 1463.[235] This devotion which *Youth 2000* wishes to inspire in Catholic youth has its origins in the apparitions of Mary and is centered on the worship of the Eucharist. The pattern again becomes clear. The spiritual maturity of Catholic youth is linked to worshipful 'prayer around' the Eucharist, devotion to Mary through the Rosary, and fidelity to the teachings of the Pope. The Pope, the apparitions of Mary, and the Eucharist. The Beast, the False Prophet, and the Image. The power of three.

Pope Paul VI, in his 1965 Encyclical *Mysterium Fidei*, about the Holy Eucharist, wrote the following prayer:

> "May the Most Blessed Virgin Mary from Whom Christ Our Lord took the flesh which under the species of bread and wine 'is contained, offered, and consumed,' ...intercede before the Father of mercies so that from this same faith in and devotion toward the Eucharist may result and flourish a perfect unity of communion among all Christians."[236]

Yet Pope Paul VI was himself a devout follower of the apparitions of Mary and was an active proponent of the Marian devotion that the apparitions have prescribed: the Rosary and the Brown Scapular.[237] It is through these devices that Mary is purported to intercede for us. Therefore, Paul VI's call for Marian intercession necessarily involves an appeal to the apparitions of Mary themselves. Notice the pattern that develops from this. The pope calls upon Mary to intercede for us and to aid us in our worship of the Eucharist. The Pope, the apparitions of Mary, and the Eucharist. The Beast, the False Prophet, and the Image. The power of three.

The pattern here is as heartbreaking as it is frightening. Millions of people around the world are presently obeying the demands of the apparition and the pope to worship the bread of the altar. Millions have heard and are obeying the false gospel being taught by the apparitions of Mary and the pope. But since when have the *people of God* been instructed to bow before

---

[235] Ball, pp. 117-20

[236] Pope Paul VI, Encyclical Letter *Mysterium Fidei*, September 3, 1965

[237] *Blue Army Cell Manual*, pg. 9. Paul VI, at the 1967 International Marian Congress, quoted from Pius XII who voiced the same sentiments in his Epistle *Neminem Profecto Latet*, AAS 42(1950):390

graven images? Since when have they been instructed to worship what is made by human hands? Since when have they been instructed to worship it in secret? The answer is simple: *they never have been.* And since when has God encouraged such behavior in His children? This answer is simple, too: *Never.* True Christians will not honor the demands of the Beast and the False Prophet to worship the Image.*

But the Papacy and the apparitions have taught Catholics to do exactly that. This emphasis on consecration or 'conversion' to the apparitions of Mary, absolute submission to the pope, and faithful adoration of the Eucharist is consistent in all of the apparitions I have been able to study--from Agreda in 1617, to Fátima in 1917, to Medjugorje, the apparitions of which began in 1981 and continue today. They repeatedly emphasize these three points, which together make up the substantive prophecy of Revelation 13 (See Table 2, pg. 138). Pope after pope has bestowed blessings, doctrines and messianic attributes on the apparitions of Mary. Pope after pope has affirmed the need to worship the Eucharist, and during the Inquisitions, failure to obey resulted in financial isolation, torture, and death for a great number of true Christians. Many a saint was slain because he wished to honor God's holy law, to adore Him alone instead of the bread of the altar. Many a saint was tortured for her desire to worship God instead of bowing to the Image of the Beast. The legacy of the Gospel preserved for Christians today was bought at the expense of the saints of the previous centuries, and much of their blood was spilled so that God's name would not be defiled at the hands of the Beast and his False Prophet.

This may seem to be quite a statement by itself, but this is something that the Church of Jesus Christ has suspected for centuries. I am only voicing an opinion that has been considered a distinct possibility since the oppression of Protestant Christianity during the Inquisitions. Many men for hundreds of years have pointed out the interesting coincidence that the Papacy should be seated on a city of seven hills--a city known in the Scriptures as Babylon--and oppress the holy ones of God. They have pointed out the interesting coincidence that the popes speak blasphemy against the Most High by claiming that they "hold upon this earth

---

* Revelation 13:8, 20:4

the place of God Almighty,"[238] claiming to be God in His own Temple, the Church of Jesus Christ. Many theologians have speculated about these and many other coincidences for centuries. They have discussed these and other characteristics of the Beast in such great detail, and have so often associated such characteristics with the Papacy, that I have to this point avoided those topics altogether for fear that they have been worn thin by centuries of speculation. Indeed, just to address those issues by themselves would often be sufficient to lose an audience. So I have remained focused on the subject of this book: Eucharistic worship and how it parallels the prophecies of Revelation 13:11-18 when considered in light of the Papacy and the apparitions of Mary.

Taking the prophecies one by one, the similarities between the Beast and the False Prophet, and the Papacy and the apparitions of Mary become remarkably apparent. Do the apparitions of Mary appear like 'a lamb' but speak like 'a dragon'? Do they receive their authority from the Papacy? Do they work many miracles, even to make the fire of heaven come down to earth as men look on? Have the apparitions of Mary, by the authority of the Papacy, brought an image to life and given it the power of speech? Was the Eucharist, through the Inquisitions, given the power to demand that anyone who refused to worship it be put to death? Did the Eucharist strike fear in the hearts of all, great and small alike, causing them to receive a mark on their forehead and hands? Did those who refused to worship the Eucharist lose the right to engage in business and financial transactions through the seizure of their property? Remarkably, the answer to all of these questions is Yes.

There are, however, two more characteristics from Revelation 13 that I wish to address but cannot do so in the context of Eucharistic Worship. One characteristic is the Number of the Beast: 666. The issue of the Number is problematic because without it, no one can prove the Beast's identity. And it is problematic because that Number has so many times been proposed to identify a candidate for the title Antichrist that the

---

[238] *The Great Encyclical Letters of Pope Leo XIII*, (New York, Cincinnati, Chicago: Benziger Brothers, Printers to the Holy Apostolic See, ©1903) pg. 304. This statement was made in Leo XIII's Encyclical Letter of June 20, 1894.

Table 2: Revelation 13 and the Power of Three

13:11	Then I saw another beast… it had two horns like a lamb's but spoke like a dragon.	Apparitions appear as the lovely Mary, yet teach a gospel of falsehood
13:12	It wielded all the authority of the first beast…	Apparitions have received all of their authority from the Papacy's proclamations of Marian doctrines
13:13	It performed great signs…	Apparitions have always worked amazing miracles and wonders
13:13	…even making fire come down from heaven to earth in the sight of everyone.	Apparitions have since 1917 been making the sun appear to drop out of the sky to the earth in front of very large crowds of people
13:14	…telling them to make an image for the beast…	Apparitions have always instructed followers to worship the Eucharist, 'made with human hands,' and clearly in honor of papal doctrines
13:14	…who had been wounded by the sword and revived.	See Appendix 2
13:15	It was then permitted to breathe life into the beast's image…	Apparitions have for centuries caused the Eucharist to bleed and even pulsate with blood. The life of the flesh is in the blood (Leviticus 17:11)
13:15	…so that the beast's image could speak…	Apparitions for centuries have also been causing the Eucharist to speak to those in adoration
13:15	…and [could] have anyone who did not worship it put to death.	The Tribunals of the Inquisitions were the means by which this was enforced
13:16	It forced all the people, small and great, rich and poor, free and slave…	The history of the Inquisitions indicate that everyone feared the Tribunals. *Everyone.*
13:16	…to be given a stamped image on their right hands or their foreheads…	God's design was that the Passover ritual would mark His people this way, though He never intended the bread to be worshipped. The mark is given, nonetheless, only the wrong mark
13:17	…so that no one could buy or sell except one who had the stamped image…	The Inquisitions clearly enforced these very restrictions against those who would not worship the Eucharist
13:18	…for it is a number that stands for a person. His number is six hundred and sixty-six.	See Appendix 1

mere mention of it discredits even the most credible research. I am not immune to these problems. If I do not provide the Number, I have proven nothing. But if I do provide it, I discredit all the work I have done so far because my conclusions could easily be considered the product of idle speculation. For this reason, I have left the discussion on the Number of the Beast for a later section, Appendix 1.

The other characteristic is the Mortal Head Wound, and it is addressed in Appendix 2 because a discussion on the Head Wound necessarily involves issues that are not directly related to the Eucharist and the apparitions. The reader may consider these evidences at whatever time is appropriate.

These issues aside, I remain focused on the three main figures of Revelation 13: the Beast, the False Prophet and the Image. The historical actions of the Papacy, the apparitions of Mary and the Eucharist all provide sufficient evidence to support my position. After all, how many false teachers in history have brought to life and given the power of speech to an image which honors the teachings of a man from Rome--an image which expands on God's Passover and therefore makes a mark on the hand and forehead of whomever partakes of it and worships it? How many men sit enthroned in Rome and have a spiritual accomplice who works miracles and even makes the fire of heaven come down to earth in the sight of everyone? How many spiritual false prophets have there been in the world who owe their authority, purpose and power to the only Roman who could give it to them? The answer: Not many. And the evidence provided herein is certainly worthy of consideration. One coincidental fulfillment of Revelation 13 makes the allegations a curiosity. Two coincidences make them a point of interest. But how many does it take before the evidence is no longer considered coincidence? I will leave that decision to the reader, as I dare not elevate myself by proclaiming these things as doctrine. Belief in these allegations, severe as they are, is most emphatically *not* required of Christians, but Christians should be aware of these 'coincidences' before we rush to join in common worship with Roman Catholics. And we should consider the profound spiritual implications of worshipping such an image as the Eucharist before calling Roman Catholics our brothers and sisters in Christ.

Consorting with the Beast

Lost sheep were my people
their shepherds misled them,
straggling on the mountains;
From mountain to hill they wandered,
losing the way to their fold.
--*Jeremiah 50:6*

IT was in his first letter to Timothy that Paul warned us of a day when believable men who had received the doctrines of demons would come into the fold attempting to deceive. He wrote:

> "Now the spirit explicitly says that in the last times some will turn away from the faith by paying attention to deceitful spirits and demonic instructions..."[239]

In light of the apparitions of Mary, and in light of the worship of the Eucharist, one can see how well-intentioned people who are deceived by 'demonic instructions' are trying to mislead the elect. And I would like to point out the grave danger to which the Christian Church has unwittingly exposed itself; indeed, we have begun to pay attention to 'deceitful spirits and demonic instructions' as we join hands with our Catholic 'brethren' without fully realizing that they themselves have been deceived by demonic instruction through the apparitions of Mary, miracles of the Eucharist, and the teachings of the Papacy.

---

[239] 1 Timothy 4:1-3

One perfect example of the attempt to establish an unbiblical unity with Roman Catholicism is the work of Charles Colson in his book, *Kingdoms in Conflict*. I read (and *enjoyed*) this book as a very young Christian, and was impressed with Colson's eloquence as well as his desire to see Christians striving together for social justice and social change. One story in particular affected me deeply: that of the 1986 February Revolution in the Philippines, the famous 'bloodless coup' through which Corazon Aquino took her rightfully elected position as president. And how did this bloodless coup come about? Millions of unarmed civilians had come to the aid of the poorly armed Aquino loyalists, generals Enrile and Ramos. This was no small act of bravery considering that Ferdinand Marcos' military regime was still well-fortified. The people poured out into the streets in support of Aquino, and they did so at the instruction of their leader, Jaime Cardinal Sin. He told the people to help Enrile and Ramos: "Protect them, and bring them food." This was indeed a people's revolution, and by the time Marcos' tanks arrived to force the rebels to stand down, there were no fewer than two million people praying, singing and, most importantly, defying the heavily armed and oppressive military force. Charles Colson describes the dramatic events that ended in a nonviolent standoff between the established military and the faithful millions who offered their lives to protect their freedom and defend Enrile and Ramos:

> "Within thirty minutes two million people were on the streets. Unarmed, often gathered as church groups, they simply waited, listening to their radios, praying, and singing through the long night. ...The next day Marcos's troops began to come. One long column of tanks and trucks carried a regiment of marines. ...But just as the lead tank reached the first kneeling bodies--many of them priests and nuns--it stopped. For just a moment there was virtual silence. Then the crowd let out a prolonged cheer. The top of the tank opened and a helmeted, bemused soldier poked his head out, looked around at the masses of happy people, and shrugged his shoulders, as though to say, 'What can we do about this?' By Monday morning there were dozens of such tanks on the streets all around the military camps, stopped not by antitank missiles

> but by the bodies of praying Filipinos. …On Tuesday Marcos fled the country, defeated."[240]

The 'bloodless coup' was indeed an event to inspire the Christian mind and restore faith in the power of prayer. I was truly encouraged by the events Colson recorded, and his summary was equally encouraging:

> "A courageous cardinal, the Philippine church, and two million ordinary citizens opened a crack of light in the dark canopy that envelops so much of planet earth. …What is so remarkable about the story of the Philippines is that millions of people believed more in the power of prayer than in the power of politics; they believed that the message 'repent, be converted, and trust in Jesus' could topple even an authoritarian leader. They believed their deliverance was spiritual."[241]

To me, as a young Christian, this was a remarkable story. And since I had been Catholic all of my life, I was especially pleased to read such an amazing account of Catholics portrayed as true Christians. Colson had my admiration, my respect and my confidence.

But six years later I discovered that Colson had only told me half of the story. In *Kingdoms in Conflict*, Colson praised the efforts of those two million praying believers and spoke of the strange look on the faces of soldiers as they exited their tanks in seeming exasperation. But what Colson did not say in *Kingdoms in Conflict* is which prayer those two million believers were praying and why those soldiers looked so confused when they got out of their armed vehicles. What Colson did not say, and should have, was perhaps the most telling aspect of the bloodless coup of 1986.

Bud Macfarlane, Sr., an avid proponent of the apparitions of Mary, is described as being "one of the top experts, if not *the* top

---

[240] Colson, Charles, with Vaughn, Ellen Santilli, *Kingdoms in Conflict*, (A copublication of William Morrow and Zondervan Publishing House, ©1987) pp. 325-7

[241] Colson, pp. 332-3

expert, on this subject in the country."[242] This expert on Marian apparitions fills in the details that Charles Colson withheld in his story about the February Revolution:

> "I was with some Bishops in Washington..., three of them from the Philippines, who all attested to fact of the great crowds that were going there [to Agoo, Philippines, an apparition site]. And they also told me that the visionary had not only [had] an apparition of the Blessed Mother, but saw a tall gray-haired elderly priest next to her. When he asked the Blessed Mother who that was, she said 'That is father Patrick Peyton.' Father Peyton, as you know is the founder of the Family Rosary and the slogan, 'The family that prays together, stays together,' and 'A world at prayer is a world at peace.' And it is not a well-known fact that father Peyton had gone to the Philippines and organized a tremendous Rosary rally in December prior to the January(sic) bloodless coup in which the Marcos government was overthrown, and that two million people were at that Rosary rally in Manila. And then during the coup when the soldiers in their tanks were advancing towards the people, Our Blessed Mother appeared over the crowd and said, 'Do not shoot my children,' to the soldiers who got out of their tanks and stopped. Now the bishops told me that they had been told this by numerous soldiers recounting [the story], and Cardinal Sin is on record saying that he had also been told by the soldiers of Our Lady's apparition intervention in the Philippines."[243]

Perhaps you can appreciate the surprise I felt when I heard this. It had been six years since I read *Kingdoms in Conflict*, but I had not forgotten the details of that coup. Yet these two million people did not, as Colson asserted, "believe that the message 'repent, be converted, and trust in Jesus,' could topple even an authoritarian leader." Instead, they believed what the apparitions

---

242 Macfarlane, Sr., Bud, M.I., of The Mary Foundation, from the tape, "Update on Marian Apparitions," on March 25, 1992 at Sacred Heart Catholic Church, Wadsworth, OH. Emphasis in original

243 Macfarlane, Sr., Bud, M.I., from his speech, "The Coming Tribulations," on August, 7, 1993, Westlake, Ohio, delivered to a group of Mary Foundation friends and benefactors. Brackets added for clarity

of Mary have been teaching for centuries--that the Rosary is their greatest weapon:

> "Dear children, today I call you to begin to pray the Rosary with a living faith. That way I will be able to help you."[244]

> "You have the most powerful weapon on earth at your fingertips--the Rosary."[245]

Those two million people at the prayer meeting, the majority of whom were Catholic, were not trusting in Jesus to save their country from destruction. They were trusting in Mary, or at least in an apparition that claimed to be her. And the soldiers did not exit their tanks out of respect for the piety of the civilian protesters, as Colson asserted. They exited their tanks in bewildered confusion because they had seen the apparition defending its followers. These people had been praying to Mary and trusting in her to deliver them; and just as if it had been conjured up by their prayers, the apparition of Mary immediately came to their defense. And Charles Colson *should* have known this since he met with Cardinal Sin at the Cardinal's own home in Manila in November of 1986--only nine months after the February Revolution. In fact, Colson explains that he and Jaime Sin had become "fast friends" at an earlier meeting, and much of the information Colson related in his rendition of the February Revolution he obtained from Jaime Sin himself.[246] It is unfortunate that this vital information is not to be found in *Kingdoms in Conflict*, for in his book, Colson urges us to take on a clearly unequal yoke with people who have been deceived by demons.* For our part, we must understand that what happened in the Philippines in February of 1986 is not evidence that justifies yoking ourselves with Catholics for social change, as Colson clearly believes. For while we may freely attribute the peaceful

---

244 *Words From Heaven*, pg. 191. Message of June 12, 1986
245 *Holy Love: Messages from Our Blessed Mother Leading Souls to Holiness*, pg. 11. Message of June 10, 1993
246 Colson, pp. 327-8
* Remarkably, Colson responded to these allegations by saying, "So, while I was not aware of the events that you report, my basic conclusions would be the same."(Letter to White Horse Publications, 5/24/95)

February Revolution to the power of God since He is in control of all things, we can also say with confidence that it was not because the Roman Catholic Filipinos had asked *Him* to help them.

I have been equally disappointed with what I saw in 1980 from the most widely-known Protestant evangelist alive today: Billy Graham. I do not wish to discredit Billy Graham Ministries, so let me make this clear now. Billy Graham has steadfastly made God's Word available to a dying world and I dare not criticize his work. His ministry has successfully brought the Gospel of Jesus Christ to more people than I could ever hope to. What I do question, however, is Mr. Graham's discernment. Early in 1980, after John Paul II's visit to the United States from the first through the seventh of October of 1979,[247] the Reverend Billy Graham wrote a lengthy article for the *Saturday Evening Post* about the papal visit. He did not spare his praises for the pope, as he said, "John Paul II has emerged as the greatest religious leader of the modern world, and one of the greatest moral and spiritual leaders of this century."[248] Graham continued in this fashion for pages, and then concluded,

> "During his visit to America Pope John Paul II was indeed a bridge builder, and that is something that this world desperately needs. In a world which often seems to have lost its way, his voice will continue to remind us of our responsibilities to each other--and to God."[249]

I do not disagree with Mr. Graham* that the world needs a guiding light, but I do know that John Paul II is not it. What Billy Graham did not mention in his review of the pope's visit is that

---

[247] *US News & World Report*, October 8, 1979, volume 87, number 15, "America Meets John Paul," pp. 18-20

[248] *The Saturday Evening Post*, February 1980, vol. 252, number 1, Graham, Billy, "The Pilgrim Pope: A Builder of Bridges," pp. 72-5,89

[249] *The Saturday Evening Post*, February 1980, pg. 89

* Apparently, Mr. Graham's position on John Paul II has not changed in the last 14 years. Regarding the recent selection of *Time*'s Man of the Year, Graham said of John Paul II, "He'll go down in history as the greatest of our modern Popes. He's been the strong conscience of the whole Christian world." (*Time*, Volume 144, Number 26, December 26, 1994/January 2, 1995, "Empire of the Spirit," pp. 53-57)

just months before his arrival in America, John Paul II visited the shrine of Knock Ireland to celebrate the 100th anniversary of the apparitions there. This is reported by Bob and Penny Lord in their book, *The Many Faces of Mary*:

> "Pope John Paul II in 1979 ...came as a pilgrim to Knock. He celebrated Mass in the Basilica, anointed the sick, and went to the Shrine to pray. He also presented to Knock Shrine a gold rose, in commemoration of the gold rose that Mary wore during her apparition."[250]

Only months before his visit to America, John Paul II consecrated the graven bread during the Sacrifice of the Mass, held it aloft for people to worship it, and then validated the appearances of a demonic force of evil by presenting the apparition shrine with a gold rose. The pope erected an image for worship, bestowed his blessings on the apparitions of Mary and then came to America 'to remind us of our responsibilities to each other--and to God.'

As I said, I do not question Billy Graham's ministry. I only question his discernment. He should have known better than to advocate the actions of the pope, because this information that I have presented is as easy to find as it apparently is to overlook. Some of our greatest evangelical leaders are doing just that. Billy Graham called his article "The Pilgrim Pope," in reference to John Paul II's many travels. But John Paul's journeys have not been limited merely to evangelical missions in non-Catholic countries. Rather, they are interspersed between pilgrimages to Marian and Eucharistic shrines--something that is public knowledge and something that Mr. Graham should have known about before he instructed us that John Paul II is the 'greatest religious leader of the modern world.' After carrying the Eucharist in a procession for worship in Rome on the Feast of Corpus Christi on June 14 of 1979,[251] John Paul II visited Knock, Ireland, on August 21, 1979, to honor the apparition of Mary. He then visited America in October of 1979, and on September 14, 1980, visited Siena, Italy, to worship a miraculous Eucharist

---

250 Lord, *The Many Faces of Mary*, pp. 125-6

251 Lord, *This is My Body, This is My Blood: Miracles of the Eucharist, Book I*, (Westlake Village, CA: Journeys of Faith, ©1986) pg. 8

there.[252] He later went on pilgrimages to Fátima, Portugal, on May 13, 1982,[253] and to Lourdes, France, on August 15, 1983.[254] These last two locations are among the most prominent and most frequented apparition sites in the world, and John Paul II's visits there were made publicly. Before Mr. Graham sings the lauds of the Roman Pontiff, he needs to learn what John Paul II really means when he says that we should demonstrate our piety by worshipping the Eucharist and being devoted to Mary. And Pope John Paul II needs to hear and respond to the true Gospel of Jesus Christ.

But Billy Graham and Charles Colson are not the exceptions. On March 29, 1994, a document was compiled under the title, *Evangelicals and Catholics Together: The Christian Mission in the Third Millennium.*[255] The name is quite benign, but the contents ring of a very dangerous tone--one that betrays the very foundations of Biblical Christianity and mocks the Gospel of Jesus Christ. For it is in this document, known also as the *Catholic-Evangelical Accord,* that noted evangelicals have set aside Paul's admonition in 1 Corinthians 6--that we not be unequally yoked with non-Christians--in favor of the politically acceptable option of calling the unsaved by the cherished title 'Christian.'

It would be unfair, however, to suggest that some caution was not shown with regard to several of the issues on which there is extreme variance between the beliefs of the Protestant and Catholic participants in the *Accord.* For example, the authors of the document were very astute in pointing out that Catholics and Evangelicals disagree about whether or not church is "an integral part of the Gospel or …[is] a communal consequence of the Gospel," whether the sacraments are symbols of grace or a means of obtaining grace, and whether or not the Lord's Supper is a Eucharistic sacrifice or a memorial meal.[256]

---

252 Lord, *This is My Body, This is My Blood, Book I*, pg. 56

253 Zimdars-Swartz, pg. 217

254 Duggan, pp. 152-4

255 The surprising list of signatories to this document is found in Appendix 3

256 *Evangelicals and Catholics Together: The Christian Mission in the Third Millennium*, March 29, 1994, pg. 10. Brackets added for clarity

But while the authors of the document acknowledged such unresolved issues as these, they never suggested, for example, that those who *did* consider their church attendance to be part of the Gospel or who *did* trust in the sacraments for their salvation, were unsaved. Instead, they merely promised to try to understand one another more completely.[257] This is a mockery of the Gospel of Jesus Christ. And for what? The only benefit to be obtained by such an agreement is an appearance of unity where in fact there is none, and indeed where none was intended by Christ.

But this is only a part of my concern. On page 21 of the document a most startling statement is made:

> "We seek and pray for the conversion of others, even as we recognize our own continuing need to be fully converted."

'Our own continuing need to be fully converted'? How is it that the Christian authors of the document were so easily confused about the difference between such Biblical concepts as Salvation, which occurs only once, and Sanctification, which is a lifelong process? Christians do not need to be converted daily but are converted only once.[258] After having been saved, Christians are continually being sanctified by growing in their understanding of His Word.[259] It is truly shocking then that great evangelical men would either ignore or fail to recognize the incorrect teaching of salvation as a continuing, unfinished process, which is how it is reflected in the document. But where do such teachings find their origins? From none other than the apparitions of Mary. It was on February 25, 1993 that the apparition of Mary in Medjugorje taught the same spiritual lesson to the visionaries there:

> "You cannot say that you are converted, because your life must become a daily conversion."[260]

To the contrary, a true Christian can confidently assert that he or she is converted and saved, and the true Christian can and

---

257 *Evangelicals and Catholics Together,* pg. 11

258 See 1 John 5:17 and Acts 16 31, among others

259 See John 17:17 and 2 Peter 1:19, among others

260 *The Mir Response: A Loving Answer to Our Mother's Call,* Volume 5, No. 2, April/May 1993 edition, inside front cover. Message of 2/25/93

should make this assertion without doubt. Not so according to the apparitions, and not so according to some of America's greatest evangelicals. I have no doubt that the Evangelical signers of the document recognize that the Christian is considered fully justified by faith, and I have no doubt that the Catholic signers believe quite the opposite--that they are never fully justified before God in this life. But herein lies the problem. Note the careful selection of the word 'conversion' in the *Catholic-Evangelical Accord*. By using this word, the Evangelical is free to read the statement, '...even as we recognize our own continuing need to be fully *sanctified*,' while the Catholic can read it '...even as we recognize our own continuing need to be fully *justified*.' In this manner all of the signatories can walk away under the appearance of agreement when in fact there is none at all. The Evangelical signers should have recognized this deception immediately and withheld their signatures.

So why *did* such men as Charles Colson, Bill Bright, J.I. Packer and Pat Robertson, among many others, agree to sign the document, and thereby appear to agree that Christians are never fully saved in this life? Paul gives us a simple answer: "Now the Spirit explicitly says that in the last times some will turn away from the faith by paying attention to deceitful spirits and demonic instructions." Whether in full knowledge or by deceit, these men have signed up to a doctrine that is devilish in its origins. This is not to say that these men are not Christians, but rather to call their teachings to question, and their discernment as well.

In saying this I do not wish to pronounce judgment against my own brothers in Christ. Bill Bright, Billy Graham, J.I. Packer, Pat Robertson and Charles Colson have all participated in Biblical ministries of excellence. I would be a foolish man to assert that somehow I had acquired a greater wisdom than they. Obviously these men know God personally through Jesus Christ and love Him deeply. However, since they are men of such great wisdom and are quite clearly involved in ministries of teaching, I call upon the words of James 3:1,

> "Not many of you should become teachers, my brothers, for you realize that we will be judged more strictly."

I do not claim to know what is in the hearts of these men, teachers of the Word as they are. However, because of the nature of their gift and because of the requirements of their positions, I can say this: *they ought to know better*. I do not offer that with any intended disrespect, but these men, whatever their intentions, have encouraged us to yoke ourselves with people who have followed apparitions of Mary, worshipped a piece of bread, and otherwise pursued activities that are wholly abominable to God. These men, with all of their ecumenistic intentions, have fallen short of their call because they have failed to recognize the most clever deception Satan has ever devised: the false Roman doctrines of Eucharistic Worship, Marian devotion and Papal primacy. And in their failure to recognize the deception, these great men have inadvertently asked us to accept without further question the false gospel of demons and the idolatrous practice of Eucharistic adoration.

But, again, they are not alone. Thousands of evangelical pastors have committed the same error. How many times have Protestant pastors applauded the work of our Christian 'sister,' Mother Teresa? A kind-hearted, generous woman, I do not dispute, but in consideration of her following statement, with whom would you conclude that she enjoys a personal relationship?

> "Mary is our Advocate who prays to Jesus for us. It is only through the Heart of Mary that we come to the Eucharistic Heart of Jesus."[261]

Does Mother Teresa have a personal relationship with the Jesus Christ of the Bible? With Mary? With a piece of bread? From her statement, it is hard to tell, but her practice of worshipping the Eucharist for one hour each day[262] certainly suggests that she enjoys the latter two of the three. Though I do not question Mother Teresa's love of the poor, I must contend with her on the position she takes regarding the mediation of Mary and the worship of the Eucharist. Mother Teresa is not preaching a Gospel of salvation through Christ, but thousands of

---

261 *Signs of the Times*, Volume 5, Number 4, September/October/November 1993, "Marian News Update: Lay Group Seeks New Marian Dogma," pp. 6-7

262 *Signs of the Times*, Volume 6, Number 2, Volume 6, Number 2, April/May/June 1994 edition, "Message From Mother Teresa of Calcutta," pg. 19

pastors refer to her yearly as if she is. Tony Campolo epitomizes this problem when he says,

> "And if you become lovers of people in the name of Christ, everything about you will change. Your lifestyle will change. It will. The stuff you buy, the stuff that you want out of life will change. Let me put it simply. [If] you become a lover of God and a lover of people, you won't be able to become a yuppie. ...You say, 'What do you want to do? Do you want to turn us all into Mother Teresas?' Yeah! Yeah, that's what I would like."[263]

As much as I admire Mother Teresa for her work with the poor, and as much as I admire Tony Campolo for preaching that we need to consider our possessions lost for the sake of Christ, I cannot approve of Campolo's message that we should be like Mother Teresa. For all practical purposes, he has validated the ministry of a woman who worships a piece of bread and trusts in Mary as her mediator between herself and the Eucharist. Tony Campolo should know better. He needs to learn what Mother Teresa really believes about worshipping the Eucharist and about the role of Mary in salvation before he commits us all to her errors. And Mother Teresa needs to hear and respond to the true Gospel of Jesus Christ.

Perhaps my assertions have been strong, but I believe it is necessary to call our teachers to account. I must appeal to these leaders in the Church and I must do so publicly. When Paul first realized that Peter was compromising the doctrine of justification by faith alone, he made a public confrontation of Peter for the sake of "the truth of the gospel."[264] I make the same appeal, asking these men to qualify their positions and *please* to stand down from their ecumenical advances because the same doctrine is at stake. The teaching of the Catholic Church on justification by works has not changed in the last 500 years, but these men who would have us accept the Catholic Church as a Christian

---

263 Campolo, Tony, "Take the Challenge! The Kingdom of Ticky-Tack: Being A Live Christian in a Dead World," Produced and directed by Peter Larson. A Zondervan Video Release, ©1992. All rights reserved. Brackets added for clarity

264 Galatians 2:14

denomination are acting in a manner which suggests that it has. And equally disturbing is the result that these respected evangelical leaders have inadvertently caused the Church of Jesus Christ to condone Eucharistic Worship and belief in the visions of Mary as acceptable Christian practices. These teachers who would have us join hands in fellowship with those who follow the apparitions of Mary and worship the Eucharist are causing the elect to believe there can be Biblical unity where there should be none at all. And the result is that the beautiful Bride of Christ is unwittingly beginning to walk hand in hand with the Beast.

Ancient Tradition

I have applied these things to myself and Apollos for your benefit, brothers, so that you may learn from us not to go beyond what is written...
--1 Corinthians 4:6a

PERHAPS the most peculiar attribute of the antichrist is that he should be able to trace his teachings back as far as the first century, a time when the New Testament was being written. Because of this ability, the antichrist will be in the interesting position of being able to suggest that his teachings were the original teachings of the Church. Paul wrote in the first century, referring to the antichrist, that "the mystery of lawlessness is already at work,"[265] and the apostle John repeated this warning, stating that "the spirit of the antichrist ...in fact is already in the world."[266] Since this is true, and the spirit of the antichrist, that 'mystery of lawlessness,' was already at work in the first century, it becomes rather important for Christians to know that the truth of the Gospel is based, not on what the so-called 'Fathers of the Church' believed, but on what is written in the Bible. This means that Christians need to be immersed in Scripture so that no one can deceive them merely by establishing the historicity of a doctrine. Since it is absolutely necessary that a Christian doctrine have its origins in the Bible, what should it matter that a doctrine can be traced back to the time of the apostles? Peter, after all, warned that "there will be false teachers among you, who will introduce destructive heresies."[267] And

---

[265] 2 Thessalonians 2:7

[266] 1 John 4:3b

[267] 2 Peter 2:1

Jesus Himself, in Revelation 2:2 commended the Ephesians for their ability to discern false apostles, meaning that people calling themselves Christians were wrongly attempting to wield apostolic authority--and thereby to propose false doctrines--very early in the life of the Church.

If the Ephesians could not trust the extrabiblical teachings of some first century teachers, what should it matter that certain beliefs or doctrines can be traced back that far, or to more recent "Doctors of the Church"? If a great man like Aquinas taught the false Gospel of the Catholic Church, then his own teachings invalidate his testimony in spite of the appearance of great wisdom in other matters. Regardless of the exalted position which philosophers and preachers may reserve for him, Aquinas, among many other 'Church Fathers,' quite simply taught the Gospel of Rome and encouraged people to bow down and worship the image of the antichrist which, I believe, we were warned about in Revelation 13. And since the false doctrines of the antichrist ought to be traceable to the first century, as Paul and John clearly suggest, then we need to be cautious of those who propose questionable doctrines, even if they can trace the origins of those doctrines back to the first few years of the life of the Church. The Catholic Church claims that it has preserved the doctrines of Christianity through the "continuous line of succession" from the apostles,[268] yet often will defer to ancient Tradition to explain the origins of its beliefs and practices. Which means that the Catholic Church is doing no more than what Paul's and John's teachings indicate that the antichrist would be able to do anyway.

One perfect example of this is the writing of Ignatius of Antioch, a first century theologian and a canonized saint of the Catholic Church. Since Ignatius died shortly after the turn of the first century (107 AD), and since he espoused a great many 'Catholic' doctrines, he is often quoted by Roman Catholic apologists to prove that the Catholic Church can indeed find the origins of its teachings in the first century. For instance, Ignatius taught that the sacraments of the Church were valid only if administered by a bishop.[269] Is there a Biblical precedent for that?

---

268 *The Catechism of the Catholic Church*, Part 1, Section 1, Chapter 1, Article 2.I, "The Apostolic Tradition," paragraph 77

269 Ignatius of Antioch, *To the Smyrnæans*, paragraph 8,
continued on next page

There is not, yet this teaching originated in the first generation after the apostles. Ignatius also taught that salvation was impossible outside of communion with the bishop:

> "God forgives all who repent, so long as their repentance turns to union with God and communion with the bishop."[270]

Ignatius' assertion that communion with the bishop is a precursor to forgiveness is untenable from a strictly Biblical standpoint. Yet it is only slightly different than the claim Pope Boniface VIII made in his famous Bull *Unam Sanctam* of November 18, 1302, when he stated that salvation was impossible outside of communion with the Bishop of Rome, the Roman pontiff:

> "Indeed we declare, announce and define, that it is altogether necessary to salvation for every human creature to be subject to the Roman pontiff.*"[271]

Is there any Biblical precedent for this? There is not, yet the precursor to this teaching can be found as early as the first century. But the early origins certainly do not justify the teaching. They merely prove that the doctrine dates from an era when the spirit of the antichrist was already in the world.

---

and *To Polycarp*, paragraph 5

270 Ignatius of Antioch, *To the Philadelphians*, paragraph 8

* Many attempts have been made throughout history to soften the impact of this profound theological assertion by Boniface VIII. It must be understood, however, that this statement was made in 1302. At the time of Boniface VIII's Bull, the Inquisitions were well underway, having received permission to use torture only 50 years earlier from Innocent IV. This was no inclusive ecumenistic statement of affection toward all Christians. It was rather an exclusive claim that only Catholics could be saved, and then only through submission to the Pope.

271 Pope Boniface VIII, Bull *Unam Sanctam*, from the revision of the text in "*Revue des Questions Historiques,*" July, 1889, p. 255. From *Select Historical Documents of the Middle Ages*, translated and edited by Ernest F. Henderson A.B., A.M., Ph.D., (London: George Bell and Sons, ©1892) pp. 435, 437

Ignatius also taught in his letter to the Ephesians that we should honor the bishop as Jesus Christ himself:

> "For if the prayer of one or two men has so much force, how much greater is that of the bishop and of the whole Church. ...It is obvious, therefore, that we ought to regard the bishop as we would the Lord Himself."[272]

Regardless of whether Ignatius was referring to the bishop of Rome or the bishop in Ephesus, his statement makes clear that the hierarchical structure of the Catholic Church, a structure which led to the Catholic doctrine on Papal primacy, was already evolving in the first century. This teaching, though it originated in the first century, is only modestly different from that of the apparition of Mary who stated in 1986 that, "The priests must follow the pope for to walk by him is to walk by my Son Himself."[273] This teaching has hardly changed in 2000 years, but that only makes it a 2000-year-old doctrine, and it serves only to prove that this doctrine was being taught at a time when the mystery of lawlessness was already at work anyway.

Further, Ignatius explained in his letter to the Smyrnæans that the Eucharist was the true flesh and blood of Jesus Christ, and to believe contrary to this was un-Christian:

> "Judgment will be meted out ...if they do not believe in the blood of Christ. ...They abstain from the Eucharist and from prayer, because they do not admit that the Eucharist is the flesh of our Savior Jesus Christ, the flesh which suffered for our sins..."[274]

Yet even Jesus and Paul freely referred to communion as mere bread after it was blessed.* Certainly this gives Christians the license they need to refer to the Communion elements as bread and wine, yet Ignatius' assertions are no different than the teachings of the apparition of Mary, who in 1986 stated that "It is

---

272 Ignatius of Antioch, *To the Ephesians*, paragraphs 5-6

273 *Our Lady Queen of Peace*, "An Urgent Appeal: Our Lady in Argentina," pg. 7. Message of October 27, 1986. Used by permission

274 Ignatius of Antioch, *To the Smyrnæans*, paragraph 6

* John 13:18 and 1 Corinthians 11:26-28

in the Eucharist that He becomes again Body and Blood."[275] And neither does it differ from the teachings of the Council of Trent, which taught that expressing an opinion to the contrary was an act worthy of excommunication:

> "If anyone shall deny that in the sacrament of the most Holy Eucharist are contained truly, really and substantially the body and blood together with the soul and divinity of our Lord Jesus Christ...--*anathema sit*."[276]

There is little doubt that these doctrines were taught as early as the first century, but that does not make them true. It only makes them old. And it only proves that the doctrines most central to the Catholic faith and most important to the apparitions were being taught at a time when the spirit of the antichrist was already in the world.

Ignatius of Antioch is also purported to teach that no one who placed his trust in Mary would be lost:

> "He who is devout to the Virgin Mother will certainly never be lost."[277]

This teaching, if it can truly be attributed to Ignatius of Antioch, is no different from that which we hear from the apparitions of Mary today, who teach that "Those who place their confidence in me will be saved."[278] This teaching is clearly errant, yet it may be traceable all the way back to the first century.

---

[275] *Our Lady Queen of Peace*, "An Urgent Appeal: Our Lady in Argentina," pg. 7. Message of June 1, 1986. Used by permission

[276] The General Council of Trent, Session XIII (1551): DS 1651

[277] *Virgin Wholly Marvelous: Praises of Our Lady from the Popes, Councils, Saints, and Doctors of the Church*, Peter Brookby, ed., (Cambridge, England: The Ravengate Press, ©1981) pg. 123. I find no evidence in his writings that Ignatius of Antioch ever voiced such a sentiment. Nonetheless, this statement is often attributed to him. See *The Mir Response,* Volume 5, Number 2, April/May 1993 issue, "Mother of Mercy," pg. 5

[278] *Our Lady Queen of Peace*, "Church Approves Messages, Weeping Statue as Supernatural," pg. 16. Message of October 13, 1973. Used by permission

Again, this does not make it true. It only makes it a very old doctrine which can be traced to a time at which the spirit of the antichrist was already working to deceive. The key issue, of course, is not whether we can trace a doctrine back to the first century, but rather whether we can trace it back to the Bible. This doctrine of *sola scriptura* has served to separate the elect from the antichrist ever since the spirit of the antichrist began its deception.

In this matter, I cannot help but to express my own personal admiration for the saints at Philadelphia in the first century. Their example is awe-inspiring to me, as is their apparent love of the Scriptures. Their obedience to the Word was beyond question and it appears that they followed Paul's instructions in Acts 20 exactly as he spoke them. After warning that 'savage wolves' would arise within the Church, Paul instructed us that God's Word would be our sure foundation and protection against falsehood:

> "I know that after my departure savage wolves will come among you, and they will not spare the flock. And from your own group, men will come forward perverting the truth to draw disciples away after them. So be vigilant and remember that for three years, night and day, I unceasingly admonished each of you with tears. And now I commend you to God and to that gracious word of his that can build you up and give you the inheritance among all who are consecrated."[279]

Notice the key elements of Paul's admonition: 1) savage wolves will arise among them, 2) these wolves will spring up attempting to pervert the truth, and 3) our vigilant adherence to the truth will depend on God and His Word. This is especially interesting in light of the fact that Ignatius of Antioch appealed to his familiarity with Paul when he wrote his letters. For example, in his letter to the Church in Ephesus, he wrote:

> "You have shared in the sacraments with Paul who was made a saint, who died a martyr, who deserved to be blessed--in whose footsteps may I be found when I reach God; in whose every letter there is a mention of you in Christ Jesus."[280]

---

[279] Acts 20:29-32

[280] Ignatius of Antioch, *To the Ephesians*, paragraph 12

Ignatius of Antioch knew how much the early Church respected Paul. Therefore his attempt to teach new doctrines was preceded by an appeal to Paul's authority. But Ignatius' teachings were not founded in Scripture, and the early Church, following Paul's instructions, knew exactly what to do. When Ignatius' teaching went beyond Scripture, the Philadelphians confronted him publicly, and it was they who caused Ignatius so much frustration when his teachings were refused for lack of Biblical support. Although Ignatius had written in his letter to the Trallians that "I have not felt myself in a position to command you as though I were an Apostle,"[281] he freely attempted to wield such apostolic authority with the church at Philadelphia and even presumed to call his own teachings the word of God:

> "I cried out in your midst and I spoke with a loud voice--with the voice of God: 'Give heed to the bishops, the priests and the deacons.' When I said this, there were those who suspected that I knew ahead of time of the schism of some among you. But He is my witness, for whom I am in chains, that I knew of this from no human lips. It was the Spirit that proclaimed these words: 'Apart from the bishop let nothing be done.'"[282]

Ignatius had attempted to go beyond the Scriptures, and even called his own words 'the voice of God.' But the Philadelphians would not have it. One paragraph later, Ignatius complained of their response to his new doctrines:

> "There are some whom I heard to say: 'Unless I find it in the documents, I do not believe in what is preached.' When I said: 'It is the written word,' they replied: 'That is what is in question.'"[283]

Remarkably, Ignatius continued in his theme by elevating *traditional* accounts of Jesus' life to the level of canon, as he countered the *sola scriptura* stand of the Philadelphians by saying

---

[281] Ignatius of Antioch, *To the Trallians*, paragraph 3

[282] Ignatius of Antioch, To the Philadelphians, paragraph 7

[283] Ignatius of Antioch, *To the Philadelphians*, paragraph 8. Quotation marks added to clarify when Ignatius is speaking in the first person as himself, and in the first person as those who disagreed with him.

"For me, Jesus Christ is the written word, His cross and death and resurrection and faith through Him make up the untampered documents."[284] Yet as early as the turn of the first century, Christians were appealing to a set of 'documents,' apart from which and in addition to which nothing was held to be authoritative, inspired and canonical. I cannot help but to express my admiration for these Philadelphians for standing their ground. It was they who were commended by Christ in Revelation 3:8 because "you have kept my word." And true to their love of the Word, it was they who caused Ignatius so much heartache for stifling his attempts at proposing false doctrines. This they did using the strength afforded them by the Holy Spirit--exactly as Paul instructed at Miletus.[*] Ignatius was attempting to teach early Christians that submission to the bishop was required for salvation, that believing in transubstantiation of the Eucharist was what makes one Christian, and that the ordinances of Christ were invalid outside of the administration of a priest or bishop. And when the Philadelphians could not find evidence for these doctrines in Paul's letters, and could find no function of a separate class of 'priests' defined in the New Testament Scriptures, they rejected the new teachings altogether, as well as Ignatius' attempt at passing himself off as a self-styled apostle. This was exactly the kind of discernment for which Jesus had applauded them in His Revelation to John, and Ignatius' mention of people who resisted his teachings is a tacit acknowledgment that the honorable belief of *sola scriptura* was alive and well in the first century Church. What Ignatius was so quick to call 'schism' was nothing less than the obedience of the early Christians who knew "not to go beyond what is written."[285]

The most telling element of Ignatius' statement, however, is not that anyone questioned his authority to propose new doctrine, but that Ignatius himself was so offended when they did. Had he been as familiar with Paul as he suggests, he certainly must have known that Paul had warned the churches of such men as he. And in their response to Ignatius, the Philadelphians had done no more than what Paul himself had instructed. He commended us to God

---

[284] Ignatius of Antioch, *To the Philadelphians*, paragraph 8
[*] Acts 20:17-38
[285] 1 Corinthians 4:6b

and to His Word, even if someone should come among the flock and attempt to deceive us. Again, I cannot help but to applaud their discernment, which was successful only because of their obedient stand on the Word.

But I did not write this with the intention of ridiculing Ignatius of Antioch. Instead, I expounded on his teaching and discussed the hurdles he encountered to make one specific point: the teachings of the Catholic Church can indeed be traced back to the first century, and Ignatius' writings are often heralded by those who wish to prove it. For example, in the introduction to the 72-volume work, *The Fathers of the Church*, the Catholic editors made the following claims specifically in reference to the very early writings of Ignatius of Antioch:

> "As for modern sectarian Christianity, the shibboleths of controversy lose their force in the face of this massive evidence. Phrases like 'corruptions in doctrine and discipline' look rather ridiculous when the 'corruptions' are traced back, in an unbroken line, from the seventh, to the fourth, to the first century. ...Yet no Latin Father was ever so strong for the hierarchic position of bishops and no modern 'Romanist' was ever more flattering in speaking of the primacy of Rome than the Syrian bishop [Ignatius] of Antioch."[286]

Indeed, Ignatius of Antioch was precisely the proponent of Catholic doctrines that the editors of *The Fathers of the Church* make him out to be. But Ignatius went further than that. In addition to proposing such characteristically Catholic doctrines so early in the life of the Church, Ignatius also has the interesting distinction of being the first theologian to refer to the Church as 'Catholic.' This he did in his letter to the Smyrnæans, saying that "...wherever Jesus Christ is, there is the Catholic Church."[287]

Ignatius' statement is an excellent reference for those who wish to prove that the Roman Catholic Church truly is a denomination of Christianity and was the only denomination in existence in the first century. And to lend further credibility to the

---

[286] *The Fathers of the Church*, volume 1, *The Apostolic Fathers*, Schopp, Ludwig, ed., (Washington, DC: The Catholic University of America Press, ©1947), pg. xi. Brackets added for clarity

[287] Ignatius of Antioch, *To the Smyrnæans*, paragraph 8

man who was the first to call the Church of Rome by the name it has adopted for itself, the 1994 *Catechism of the Catholic Church* refers to Ignatius' letters no fewer than 18 times to support its doctrines.[288] If the Catholic Church wishes to prove from extrabiblical documents (e.g., the writings of Ignatius of Antioch) that its doctrines are as old as the Christian Church itself, that is its prerogative. But the repeated reference to Ignatius of Antioch accomplishes nothing except to prove that the teachings of the Catholic Church and the name 'Catholic' were already in circulation as early as the first century. But that was not a sufficient method of establishing doctrine then, and it is certainly not a sufficient method today. And efforts to use such writings as those of Ignatius to justify extrabiblical doctrines will be a stumbling block for unity as long as there are Christians who stand on the Word alone. The disunity between Catholics and Protestants has always, and will always, come down to that.

And it seems that this troubling disunity between Catholics and Evangelicals can be traced back to the first century as well. This statement is not as ludicrous as it may sound, because Ignatius of Antioch was proposing a certain *Catholic-Evangelical Accord* of his own. Ignatius, as it turns out, loved unity above all other things, as he wrote to Polycarp, "Be preoccupied about unity, for nothing is better than this."[289] Yet this sentiment was not expressed by Paul when he confronted Peter publicly,[*] and neither was it expressed by John when he threatened to confront Diotrophes publicly.[†] Obviously these two apostles thought that there was something more important than being in communion with the bishop, and something more valuable than unity: "the truth of the gospel."[290] Not so with Ignatius. In the same breath that he questioned the *sola scriptura* stand of some first century Christians, he made the following statement:

> "Love unity. Shun schisms. Be imitators of Jesus Christ, as He is of His Father. As for me, I played my part, like a

---

[288] The 1994 *Catechism of the Catholic Church*, pp. 746-7

[289] Ignatius of Antioch, *To Polycarp*, paragraph 1

[*] Galatians 2:11-14

[†] 3 John 9-10

[290] Galatians 2:14

> mediator appointed to bring about unity. For, wherever there is division or anger, God has no place."[291]

Yet what price did Ignatius ask for the cause of unity? Too high a price, apparently. It was only two sentences after making this remark that Ignatius recorded the complaint of those who stood against him: 'Unless I find it in the documents, I do not believe in what is preached.' It is most interesting that while Ignatius was calling for unity, other Christians were willing to suffer division for the sake of the Word. In two thousand years, the Church of Jesus Christ has not changed her position. While thousands are hailing the modern *Catholic-Evangelical Accord* as a document whose time has come, an equally significant number are responding with the position for which members of the Church of Jesus Christ have fought and died for nearly 2000 years: 'Unless I find it in the documents, I do not believe in what is preached.'

Can the doctrines of the Catholic Church be traced back to the first century? They surely can, but this only proves that the Catholic Church can trace its doctrines back to a time when the 'mystery of lawlessness' was already at work. Paul and John both taught that the spirit of the antichrist was 'already in the world' in the first century, which indicates to us that tracing doctrines back that far is not sufficient for establishing Christian truth. The *sola scriptura* position of the Protestant Reformers can also be traced back to the first century. But Protestant Christians can also--and much more importantly--trace this doctrine back to the Bible, for this is the instruction that Paul passed on to the Ephesian elders as a safeguard against deception.

So the purpose of this chapter is indeed more than a critique of the writings of Ignatius of Antioch. Rather, the purpose is to concede what is already taught and believed by Catholics: that the doctrines taught by the apparitions of Mary and the Church of Rome about the worship of the Eucharist, the primacy of the Pope, and the mediation of Mary can all be traced to the first century, as can the name 'Catholic.' But that was not proof enough for the Philadelphians, and it should not be proof enough for us. If you wish to persuade me to believe a doctrine, prove it from the Bible or do not attempt to prove it at all. Did Mother

---

291 Ignatius of Antioch, *To the Philadelphians*, paragraphs 7-8

Teresa teach that Mary is our Mediatrix? To that I say the same words that so offended Ignatius: 'Unless I find it in the documents, I do not believe in what is preached.' Thomas Aquinas' hymn *Adoro Te Devote* is quoted in the 1994 *Catechism of the Catholic Church* in order to prove that Eucharistic Worship and the Sacrifice of the Mass are true Christian practices.[292] Again, I say the words that were such an effrontery to Ignatius: 'Unless I find it in the documents, I do not believe in what is preached.' Indeed, these people have preached the doctrines of the apparitions of Mary, the false prophet which is the spirit of the antichrist, a spirit that was active before the first century had even come to a close. Do the apparitions preach the ancient doctrines of the Catholic Church? Without a doubt, they do. But what is that to me? I say it again: 'Unless I find it in the documents, I do not believe in what is preached.' And should someone say that Mother Teresa and John Paul II are great spiritual leaders, and that Aquinas was a Doctor of the Church, to that I respond with another statement that was so painful to Ignatius' ears: '*That* is what is in question.'

---

[292] *The Catechism of the Catholic Church*, Part 2, Section 2, Chapter 1, Article 3.V, "The Sacramental Sacrifice: Thanksgiving, Memorial, Presence," paragraph 1381

Epilogue

If the pope be not anti-christ, he hath the ill-luck to appear so much like him.
--*Richard Baxter*

IT is clear from the Scriptures, and I think both Catholics and Protestants would agree, that Satan uses many methods to attempt to deceive the saved and the unsaved alike. He appears as an angel of light, and when he does attempt to mislead, he does so in a manner that would "deceive, if that were possible, even the elect."[293] It is true, then, that if Satan wishes to deceive even the elect, he will attempt to do so by using means and methods which are, at least on the surface, compatible with Christianity. Though many have feared through the ages that the antichrist would come with the appearance of evil, we can be assured that the Scriptures tend to portray him as a person of great charisma: "Fascinated, the whole world followed after the beast."[294] This statement by itself portrays a certain cultic personality that makes people *want* to like him. This is not something that would be likely if the antichrist were to come into the world with glowing red eyes, demanding that we sacrifice black cats to him. That would be a dead giveaway. Instead, the antichrist was prophesied to adopt a method that was much more compatible with what the people of the world consider to be 'good.' In fact, from Revelation 13, we see that the Dragon, the Beast and the False Prophet pattern themselves after the most successful worldwide evangelism program ever devised: the Christian Church.

---

293 Matthew 24:24b

294 Revelation 13:3b

We know from Jesus' words in John 8:28b that He has received authority from His Father in Heaven: "…I do nothing on my own, but I say only what the Father taught me." Jesus repeats this statement in John 12:49, saying, "I did not speak on my own, but the Father who sent me commanded me what to say and speak." He made a clear case for the fact that the Son has received authority from the Father.

And when Jesus said that He would not leave us orphaned, but would send us a Comforter, the Holy Spirit,[*] He made it clear that the Comforter would speak only what Jesus Himself had told Him to speak. The Holy Spirit, in Jesus' words, "will glorify me, because he will take from what is mine and declare it to you."[295] And though it was the Father who sent the Spirit, it was in Jesus' Name that He did so.[†]

The Spirit, on the day He descended on the apostles, did so by the authority given to Him from the One Who had come before Him. Then, having been given to the Church, the Spirit brought tongues of fire down to earth to rest on the apostles, and has since that time glorified the One Who preceded Him. He not only reminded the disciples in the young Church of what Christ had taught them,[§] but also gave witness on behalf of Jesus Christ and likewise instructed the apostles to bear witness to Christ as well.[°] He made it clear that the Spirit had received His authority from the Son.

The pattern is clear. The Father sends the Son, giving Him authority, and the Father sends the Spirit in the Name of the Son. The Spirit testifies to the Son and encourages the disciples to bear witness on His behalf, reminding them of what Jesus told them. This is a masterful work of God's marvelous design. And it is perfect.

The devil, then, wishing to imitate the Holy Trinity, does his best to appear like Them. The Dragon, the Beast, and the False Prophet of Revelation 13 adopt this imitation of the Trinity to accomplish their purposes. The Dragon gives his authority to the

---

[*] John 14:16
[295] John 16:14
[†] John 14:26
[§] John 14:26
[°] John 15:26, 27

Beast,[*] the Beast in turn gives his authority to the False Prophet,[†] and the False Prophet, having been given the authority of the Beast, brings fire down from Heaven and causes the people of the world to worship the First Beast.[§] In every way possible, this unholy trinity has mimicked the form and pattern of the Holy Trinity of God. The Trinity throughout history has demonstrated that They are the most effective and most powerful evangelizing force in all of history. Satan, desiring to lead the world astray, has no better model to follow than that.

Indeed, Satan has no other option than to attempt to imitate the One True God in order to minimize his losses. There simply was no other way for the unholy trinity of Revelation 13 "to deceive, if that were possible, even the elect."[296] Because of this, the antichrist will strive to imitate the true Church. Both Catholics and Protestants would likely agree that when the antichrist comes, he will appear so much like the true Church that it will be nearly impossible for the unregenerate heart to tell which is which.

But that leads us to a curious dilemma. To this point we have reviewed the nature of the Eucharist and the fact that it comes to life and speaks to its adorers. We have reviewed the fact that the Eucharist was the central tenet of faith in the Inquisitions and that people who refused to worship it were tortured, killed or financially constrained. We have reviewed the many apparitions which instruct people to worship the Eucharist, and we have reviewed the interesting 'coincidence' that the most common trait of any apparition from 1917 onward is to make the fire of the sun come down to earth as thousands of people look on. We have reviewed the fact that the apparitions practically begged to have the authority of the Papacy bestowed on them through Papal doctrines and proclamations. We have reviewed the fact that the apparitions have in turn taught people the doctrines of the Papacy, encouraged them to follow the pope, and erected the Eucharist to be worshipped. Again, this much both the Catholic and the Protestant would agree to: these are all historical facts based on the documents of the Catholic Church and the teachings of the

---

[*] Revelation 13:2,4

[†] Revelation 13:12, 14

[§] Revelation 13:12

[296] Matthew 24:24b

apparitions of Mary. They are all quite true, and are easily substantiated.

This means that the Catholic Church has in every way mimicked the traits of the Beast in Revelation 13. The Papacy has bestowed its authority on the apparitions who honor the popes by propagating their doctrines. However, the apparitions do not do this without first securing the blessings of the Papacy and in turn affirming the Papacy and the Eucharist which it has caused people to worship--an image that is made by human hands and is the equivalent of receiving a mark on the hands and forehead. Further, the apparitions appear "like a lamb" but speak the falsehood of Satan, all the while performing miracles, even causing the fire of heaven to come down to earth in the sight of everyone. And during the Inquisitions, the apparitions stood by and allowed the Papacy to continue to force its image worship on the people of the world. This sequence of events is a veritable duplication of the prophecies of Revelation 13.

Which leads me to my final point. We know that the antichrist will appear so much like the True Church that it will be hard to tell the difference between the two. But can we honestly assert the converse and believe it? Was the Church intended to appear so much like the antichrist that it would be difficult to tell the difference between them? That is a laughable assertion, but one we cannot avoid if we inspect the evidence and still maintain that the Roman Church is part of the Body of Christ. If the Church of Rome is the True Church of Jesus Christ, then the Bride of Christ has appeared so much like the antichrist that the people of the world will have a hard time telling who is who! If this is true, then God has befuddled us all and left us with no means of discerning truth from falsehood, meaning that our only option is to choose between two Roman dictators who each have an accomplice who works miracles and makes the fire of heaven come down to earth in the sight of men. It means that we will have to choose between two Romans who each force us to accept a mark as a result of worshipping their images. It means that we will have to decide between following one Roman whose image comes to life and speaks, and another Roman whose image does the same thing. It means that we have been left to our own devices and are compelled to decide between two forces that appear exactly the same yet have, on the one hand an inherent goodness that is too thoroughly cloaked to see, and on the other a natural evil that cannot be discerned. An impossible decision. This is the devil's best defense: that the world would not be able to discern between the True Church and his own.

But we are not left to our own devices. Satan may use imitation as his best defense, but we have the Bible as ours. There will be no two such Romans and there will be no two such false prophets and there will be no two such images to choose between. But there *is* a choice to make. A choice between a false gospel and the True Gospel of the Bible; between an image of our own making which speaks and bleeds, and the True Jesus Christ Who *really is alive* and speaks to us in His Word and *really bled* for us on the cross; between the false spirit of the antichrist who mocks the Gospel, and the Holy Spirit of God Who inspired it; between the father of lies who steals God's Word from people's hearts, and the Father of Truth, Who writes it there.

There is indeed a choice to be made and the choice is not based on what I have written, but on what God has. And I do not say this to criticize those who choose to follow the teachings of Papal Rome, who choose to bow before and worship the image the apparition of Mary has erected, who have accepted the mark of Papal Rome on their hands and foreheads. Rather, I wrote this only to establish that the choice has been made and the consequences of it are clearly spelled out in God's Word.

I began this book with a story about the Catholic salesman who wanted to sell me a car. My conversation with him drifted from topic to topic, but when we arrived at the issue of Eucharistic Worship, he became defensive. You may recall his indignation when he said, "I have been a Catholic for 46 years! If there were such a thing as Eucharistic Adoration, don't you think I would have heard of it by now?" Yet when I demonstrated to him that the documents and Popes all prove that the Catholic Church instructs us to worship the Eucharist, he conceded the point, and then added this rebuttal: "So, what if we *do* worship the Eucharist? What difference does it make?" As it turns out, his question is an important one, and it makes a great deal of difference. For it is by this means that billions of people throughout history have received the mark of the Beast without even knowing it.

What difference does it make? It is the difference between eternal life and eternal damnation. And though I cannot but mourn the souls who have wandered after the Beast, I rest secure in the assurance God has provided me, the assurance that the mark I myself once received when I worshipped the Eucharist has long since been removed by the cleansing blood of Jesus Christ. I, too, once worshipped the image of the Beast, but I bear his mark no longer. It has for some time now been replaced by the mark of my Father. And this new mark I bear is not because of *my* obedience, but because of Christ's. How can I be so sure of this? The Bible tells me so:

> "Jesus Christ… gave himself for us to deliver us from all lawlessness and to cleanse for himself a people as his own, eager to do what is good."[297]

> "For our sake he made him to be sin who did not know sin, so that we might become the righteousness of God in him."[298]

The righteousness of Christ has been transferred to my account and I bear the mark of the Beast no more, for Jesus Christ Himself has cleansed me. Perhaps I seem overconfident, but I will not change my position, for the Bible is the source of my confidence. His Word is my assurance, and is truly our best defense.

---

[297] Titus 2:13b-14
[298] 2 Corinthians 5:21

Appendix 1: The Number

By stealth and fraud he shall seize the kingdom.
--*Daniel 11:21b*

SOMETIME during the eighth century, the Papacy decided that it needed hard, documented proof of its right to rule over what had formerly been the territories of the Roman Empire. The Papacy had since the sixth century been exercising such authority, and had been doing so without question and without opposition. But the time had come to prove on paper what had been practiced in reality. The popes needed a deed of title which proved beyond a doubt that they had the license to govern over the Holy Roman Empire with all of the rights and privileges of an emperor.

So the Papacy set to work to prove what had been confidently asserted for so long, and soon produced as evidence a document that laid all questions to rest: *The Donation of Constantine*, purportedly authored by Constantine himself, Emperor of Rome from 306 to 337 AD. The document was considered authentic for hundreds of years and was held to prove that Constantine, after a miraculous recovery from a debilitating disease, ceded all of his authority and territories to Rome--and specifically to Pope Sylvester who had been ruling there at the time of Constantine's reign:

> "And when I learned these things at the mouth of the blessed Silvester, and found that I was wholly restored to health by the beneficence of blessed Peter himself, we--together with all our satraps and the whole senate, and the magnates and all the

> Roman people, which is subject to the glory of our rule--considered that, since he is seen to have been set up as the *vicar of God's Son* on earth, the pontiffs who act on behalf of that prince of the apostles should receive from us and our empire a greater power of government than the earthly clemency of our imperial serenity is seen to have conceded to them."[299]

The document proved that the Papacy, while visibly wielding its strong arm over the spiritual *and* secular affairs of the former Roman Empire, was only doing so within its rights--rights which were granted through a perfectly legal transaction from the secular authority of the Roman Empire to the spiritual authority over the same. Constantine, after the miraculous healing from St. Peter himself, recognized that the true authority over the earth belonged to the Vicar of God's Son. To deny him that power would be nothing short of defiance against the natural order that God had set up in the universe.

It was in the fifteenth century that the authenticity of the *Donation of Constantine* was first called into question. And after extensive study, it was determined that the Papacy had been acting as Emperor over the Holy Roman Empire on the authority granted to it by a forged document. Constantine had not written it after all. The Papacy had fabricated it in order to lay to rest any question of its authority. But in the 1400s the Papacy had to admit that the document was of no legal value and had no historical merit. It was a lie:

> "This document, which purports to be a deed of gift from Constantine to Pope Sylvester, was included in the 'Forged Decretals,' and it played a great part in subsequent controversies. Its authority was unquestioned till the fifteenth century, when its authenticity was impugned by many eminent churchmen and its falsity finally proved by Lorenzo Valla. It is now completely discredited."[300]

Of course, by the fifteenth century it was not feasible for the Papacy to relinquish the power that it had wrongly exercised for

---

299 *The Donation of Constantine*. Italics added

300 *Documents of the Christian Church*, Bettenson, Henry S., (London: Oxford University Press, ©1963) pg. 135

the last thousand years. But bygones were bygones and Europe went on under the rule of Papal Rome, and the embarrassment created by a forged deed of cession was left in the past. But one thing could not be left there and it has followed the Papacy to this day--his name: the Vicar of God's Son.* (See top of page 172)

Since it was the Papacy, and not Emperor Constantine, who had authored the *Donation*, it was the Papacy, and not Emperor Constantine, who first called the pope the Vicar of God's Son. In the original Latin, the language of Rome, and the language in which the *Donation* was originally penned, this name was written as *Vicarius Filii Dei*. The Vicar of God's Son.

This name has been in and out of the spotlight since the *Donation* was forged, and the Papacy cannot change the fact that it gave this name to itself. *Vicarius Filii Dei*. This name came to the surface again in 1915 when a subscriber to *Our Sunday Visitor*, a Catholic weekly periodical, wrote a letter to the editor and asked a question about the popes' miter:

> "Q: What are the letters supposed to be in the Pope's crown, and what do they signify, if anything?
> A: The letters inscribed on the Pope's mitre are these: *Vicarius Filii Dei*, which is the Latin for Vicar of the Son of

---

* Though Hardon claims that the *Donation of Constantine* "was never considered by the popes as the source of their power,"(Hardon, pg.170) he is not being entirely forthright. The popes regard God as the source of their power, but the *Donation of Constantine* was considered evidence of their right to exercise it. In the *Oxford Dictionary of Popes*, Kelly writes that the *Donation* "came to be treated as authoritative even by opponents of the papacy," and was even used by a representative of Pope Leo IX to argue "the case for the Roman primacy" during the Great Schism of 1054 AD.(Kelly, J.N.D., *The Oxford Dictionary of Popes*, (NY: Oxford University Press, ©1986) pp. 28, 148). The *Encyclopedic Dictionary of Religion* explains that "the document was used for more than 200 years against adversaries of the Holy See in both East and West." (*Encyclopedic Dictionary of Religion*, volume A-E, (Washington, DC: Corpus Publications, ©1979) pp. 1099-1100). Hardon's position is somewhat untenable if he is trying to argue that the *Donation* never received official approval by the Papacy. By default, the document was considered valid, and subsequently so was the application of the name *Vicarius Filii Dei*.

> God. Catholics hold that the Church which is a visible society must have a visible head. Christ, before His ascension into heaven, appointed St. Peter to act as His representative. Upon the death of Peter the man who succeeded to the office of Peter as Bishop of Rome was recognized as head of the Church. Hence to the Bishop of Rome, as head of the Church, was given the title, 'Vicar of Christ.'"[301]

From the day the *Donation of Constantine* was first set in ink all the way to the twentieth century--well over one thousand years--the name of the pope has been recognized by Catholics as *Vicarius Filii Dei*. Vicar of the Son of God. That is simply what the pope has been called since the foundation of the Papacy.

Now it is no surprise to anyone that certain Latin letters, commonly called Roman Numerals, have assigned numerical values. It is interesting then, that the name, Vicarius Filii Dei, when set in the form of Roman Numerals (i.e., VICARIVS FILII DEI) renders the numerical value 666:

Letter	Value	Letter	Value	Letter	Value
V	5	F	0	D	500
I	1	I	1	E	0
C	100	L	50	I	+1
A	0	I	1		=501
R	0	I	+1		
I	1		=53		
V	5				112
S	+0				53
	=112				+501
					=666

Table 3: The Number of His Name

I wish at this point to make it clear that I do not take this numerical calculation lightly. I know that there has been a '666' cult of sorts around for centuries as many have attempted to prove that their archnemesis can be assigned that number. Because of this, any discussion on the number always gives rise to skepticism

301 *Our Sunday Visitor*, April 18, 1915, Volume III, Number 51, "Bureau of Information," pg. 3. Rev. John F. Noll, Editor. Italics in original

and occasionally even reciprocated charges that the accuser's name, too, renders the value 666.

For example, Ellen Gould White, foundress and prophetess of the Seventh Day Adventist movement, was very vocal during her life about the numerical value of the name *Vicarius Filii Dei*. Catholics in response noted that her name also rendered the correct sum when written in Roman Numerals: ELLEN GOVLD VVITE. I will leave that calculation for the reader, but suffice it to say that ever since John wrote Revelation 13:18, the number 666 has been worn thin by the manipulative hands of unscrupulous eschatologists. The result is that we do the opposite of what the apostle John seemed to intend when he gave us the famous numerical criterion: "Wisdom is needed here; one who understands can calculate the number of the beast." Instead of calculating it, we discredit any attempt to do exactly what John instructed: 'calculate' it with the understanding that the number is necessary, but not sufficient, for determining the identity of the Beast. The number must necessarily be found in a person who first meets all of the other criteria of the Beast. When John wrote Revelation 13, he left the calculation of the number at the very end. For this reason, I have left the calculation for the end as well, recognizing that the calculation itself must rest first on the criteria which precede John's mention of it.

And I recognize that any speculation regarding the numerical equivalent of *Vicarius Filii Dei* would be exactly that--*pure speculation*--if there were no further evidence to back up the claims I have made. It is for this reason that the discussion on the Number is buried here in the appendices and is not found in the body of the text of *Graven Bread*. I feel that even though the number 666 is the *sine qua non* of any discussion on the antichrist, I also believe that I can back up my claims without relying on the evidence of the number alone. Therefore, the numerical value shown in Table 3 is to be understood in light of what has been discussed in the rest of the book, and not as standalone evidence for my assertions. I certainly would be as much a fool to base my conclusions on the number alone, as I would be to make these claims without this critical, albeit unduly celebrated, criterion supporting them.

Appendix 2: The Head Wound

> I saw that one of its heads seemed to have been mortally wounded, but this mortal wound was healed.
>
> --*Revelation 13:3*

ALTHOUGH a discussion on the mortal head wound of Revelation 13 is made necessary merely by the context of the discussion on the image of the Beast and the false prophet, I felt that such a tangent would distract from the expressed intentions of *Graven Bread*. For this reason, the discussion on the mortal head wound is, like that of the Number, relegated to the appendices. This is not to understate its importance, but rather to acknowledge that it will require historical evidences that are for the most part unrelated to Eucharistic worship and the apparitions of Mary. Additionally, it must be stated here that the head wound itself could be the subject of voluminous dissertations, but for the sake of brevity my theory will be expressed here in its most basic form. Like the rest of the material in *Graven Bread*, the evidences provided here are for the reader's consideration and are not provided as an independent proof of the eschatological role of the Papacy. This evidence should be considered in light of everything else that has been discussed to this point, and indeed, is built upon it.

It is a fact, according to Revelation 17:9, that the seven heads of the Beast represent seven hills and at the same time seven kings. According to Revelation 17:11, the Beast, while being an eighth king--that is, coming at some time after the seven--is really one of the original seven. Revelation 13:1-3, explains that it is one of these seven heads, or kings, which suffers the mortal head wound. This could lead into a discussion on the original date of Revelation's writing, but again, that discussion has in the past taken up entire volumes and cannot be addressed adequately in this forum.*

It is worth noting, however, that Daniel's understanding of the Roman Empire is that it would be an Iron Kingdom which would deteriorate into an Iron and Clay Kingdom after a period of united rule.† According to Daniel's interpretation of the king's vision in Daniel 2, this Iron Kingdom "shall not stay united."[302] This is an excellent description of what happened to the Roman Empire. After more than 100 years of the famous *Pax Romana*, or Roman Peace, the Roman Empire collapsed into a conflict of civil wars from which it never fully recovered. But from Julius Caesar in 49 BC to Nero's death in 68 AD, peace reigned throughout the Roman empire. Nero's successor, Galba, was not from Rome, however, and as Tacitus was so astute in recognizing, the consequences of this were devastating:

> "The brief reign of Galba was chiefly important because of the circumstances in which it came about. These were summed up by Tacitus in the introduction to *Histories*: 'A well-hidden secret of the principate had been revealed: it was possible, it now appeared, for an emperor to be chosen outside Rome.' The revelation of this secret showed the provincial garrisons their own power, incited them to display it in armed conflict one against the other, and led the way to endless military rebellions and revolutions in the centuries that lay ahead."[303]

---

* For a study in an early writing of Revelation (as early as 54 AD) see Glasgow, D.D., *The Apocalypse: Translated and Expounded*, (Edinburgh: T. & T. Clark, ©1872) pp. 38-9. Or for a study which places it in the early to mid-60s AD, see Gentry, Dr. Kenneth L. Jr., *Before Jerusalem Fell: Dating the Book of Revelation*, (Tyler, TX: Institute for Christian Economics, ©1989). Both of these scholarly works place the composition of Revelation during the reign of Nero.

† Daniel 2:40-41

302 Daniel 2:43

303 Grant, Michael, *The Twelve Caesars*, (New York: Charles Scribner's Sons, © 1975) pg. 178

From Julius Caesar to Emperor Galba, the *Pax Romana* continued uninterrupted.[304] After Galba's reign, the *Pax Romana* never returned. This leads to the interesting understanding that the Iron Period which Daniel foresaw in his vision of Daniel 2 may have been presided over by the following seven Roman emperors:

1) Julius Caesar (49-44 BC)
2) Caesar Augustus (31 BC-AD 14)
3) Tiberius (AD 14-37)
4) Gaius Caligula (AD 37-41)
5) Claudius (AD 41-54)
6) Nero (AD 54-68)
7) Galba (AD 68-69)

If it is possible that these were the seven kings to whom John referred in Revelation 17:9, and if Rome can be considered the seven-hilled city, then a fascinating correlation results.

Since Revelation 17:11 states that the Beast is an eighth king, but is really one of the seven, it follows that one of the seven should be clearly identifiable as having the same attributes of the Beast, that is, the antichrist. We need to find out which one of the seven shared those attributes, and that task is quite simple. Which of the above seven 'kings' was known for burning Christians alive? The answer is Nero. He was the first Roman emperor to persecute Christians, burning them alive 'at the stake' at night to light the streets of Rome.[305] So too was the Papacy known for burning Christians alive during the Inquisitions. The Papacy and Nero are guilty of a similar crime.

Moving on, which if any of the first seven emperors of Rome had a devotion to a female goddess figure? Again, the answer is Nero, who was known to tolerate only one cult: that of a Syrian Goddess,[306] a fascination which is closely paralleled by the devotion of the line of popes to the apparitions of Mary. Again, the Papacy and Nero share this characteristic.

---

[304] Reicke, Bo, *The New Testament Era: The World of the Bible from 500 B.C. to A.D. 100*, trans. by David E. Green, (Philadelphia, PA: Fortress, © 1968) pp. 109-110
[305] Tacitus, *Annals*, Book XV
[306] Suetonius, "Lives of the Caesars," *Nero*

To continue, were any of the first seven emperors known to have destroyed Jerusalem? Nero bears that distinction as well, as the war against Israel began under his reign. Likewise, the Papacy was responsible for Jerusalem's destruction since the Crusades which the Papacy initiated accomplished exactly that. Both Nero and the Papacy bear the shared guilt of destroying God's Holy City.

Further, were any of the first seven emperors known for a self-perception of deity? Though many of them shared this trait, Nero took it to an extreme and was thoroughly preoccupied with self-deification,[307] a trait that the so-called Vicars of Christ have also exhibited--most notably under Pope Leo XIII who stated that the popes, "hold on this earth the place of God Almighty."[308]

Finally, did any of the first seven emperors of Rome have a name with a numerical value of 666? Like the Papacy, Nero's name also provides that infamous numerical value.[309]

To summarize, then, it can be stated accurately that the Papacy has indeed exhibited character traits which demonstrate that though it is 'an eighth king,' it is really one of the seven. The Papacy in fact is really nothing more than a perpetuation of the character and purpose of Nero himself. In an unflattering description of Nero, the *Sibylline Oracles*, written sometime after 80 AD, have this to say of his character:

> "...the evil of Nero has the same three dimensions as the evil of Rome: he is morally evil, he was responsible for the destruction of Jerusalem, since the Jewish War began in his reign, and he claimed to be God."[310]

---

[307] Gentry, Dr. Kenneth L. Jr., *Before Jerusalem Fell: Dating the Book of Revelation*, (Tyler, TX: Institute for Christian Economics, ©1989) pg. 275. Taken from J.J. Collins, "Sibylline Oracles," 1:390, James H. Charlesworth, ed., *Old Testament Pseudepigrapha*, 2 vols., (New York: Doubleday & Company, Inc., © 1983), pg. 395, notes y and b2

[308] *The Great Encyclical Letters of Pope Leo XIII*, (New York, Cincinnati, Chicago: Benziger Brothers, Printers to the Holy Apostolic See, ©1903) pg. 304

[309] Gentry, pg. 199. 'Nero Caesar,' when rendered in Hebrew, gives the required sum.

[310] Gentry, pg. 275

If the author of the *Sibylline Oracles* had not clarified at the outset that the description was of Nero, one could easily believe that he had been describing the Papacy, so closely do these two Roman rulers imitate each other. 'He' is known to have been morally evil, 'he' was responsible for the destruction of Jerusalem, and 'he' claimed to be God.

With this information, the identification is complete. The Papacy, the Beast of Revelation, even though it is 'an eighth king,' is truly 'one of the seven' emperors of the once united Roman empire. Which one of the seven? Caesar Nero, of course. Not surprisingly, Nero did in fact die of a mortal head wound, self-inflicted to his neck.[311] In spite of that, his character was continued in, and mirrored by, the very lengthy line of popes who would rule in Rome after him. Nero experienced a mortal head wound, but lived on in the form of a monarchical, religio-political system that would mimic his every character flaw. This leads to the ironic yet not altogether unbelievable conclusion that the Papacy finds its origin in Caesar Nero, and not in Peter after all.

---

[311] Suetonius, "Lives of the Caesars," *Nero*

Appendix 3

Original signatories of *Evangelicals and Catholics Together: The Christian Mission in the Third Millennium*, March 29, 1994:

Dr. William Abraham, Perkins School of Theology, SMU
Dr. Elizabeth Achtemeier, Union Theological Seminary
Mr. William Bentley Ball, of Ball, Skelly, Murren & Connell
Dr. Bill Bright, Campus Crusade for Christ
Mr. Charles Colson, Prison Fellowship
Prof. Robert Destro, Columbus School of Law, Catholic University of America
Rev. Juan Diaz-Vilar, SJ, Catholic Hispanic ministries
Rev. Augustine DiNoia, OP, Dominican House of Studies
Rev. Avery Dulles, SJ, Fordham University
Rev. Joseph P. Fitzpatrick, Fordham University
Bishop William Frey, President, Trinity Episcopal School for Ministry
Prof. Mary Ann Glendon, The Law School, Harvard University
Bishop Francis George, OMI, Diocese of Yakima, WA
Dr. Os Guinness, The Trinity Forum
Dean Nathan Hatch, The Graduate School, University of Notre Dame
Dr. Kent Hill, President, Eastern Nazarene College
Dr. James Hitchcock, St. Louis University
Prof. Peter Kreeft, Boston College
Rev. Matthew Lamb, Boston College
Dr. Richard Land, Christian Life Commission, Southern Baptist Convention
Dr. Larry Lewis, Home Mission Board, Southern Baptist Convention
Mr. Ralph Martin, Renewal Ministries
Dr. Jesse Miranda, Assemblies of God
Dr. Richard Mouw, President, Fuller Theological Seminary
Msgr. William Murphy, Archdioces of Boston
Rev. Richard John Neuhaus, Institute on Religion and Public Life
Dr. Mark Noll, Wheaton College
Mr. Michael Novak, American Enterprise Institute

Mr. Brian O'Connell, World Evangelical Fellowship
John Cardinal O'Connor, Archdiocese of New York
Dr. Thomas Oden, Drew University
Prof. J. I. Packer, Regent College
Rev. Pat Robertson, Chancellor, Regent University
Dr. John Rodgers, Director, Alfred Stanway Institute for World Missions, Trinity Episcopal School for Ministry
Mr. Herbert Schlossberg, Fieldstead Foundation
Bishop Carlos A. Sevilla, SJ, Archdiocese of San Francisco
Archbishop Francis Stafford, Archdiocese of Denver
Mr. George Weigel, Ethics and Public Policy Center
Dr. John White, Geneva College

Bibliography

A Call to Peace, "Locutions from the Hidden Flower of the Immaculate Heart," published by Mir-A-Call Center, 418 Town Center, Bella Vista, Arkansas 72714

Abóbora, Lucia, *Fatima In Lucia's Own Words: Sister Lucia's Memoirs*, Kondor, Louis, SVD, ed., (Still River, MA: The Ravengate Press, ©1976)

Ashton, Joan, *The People's Madonna,* (London: Harper-Collins Publishers, ©1991)

Atlanta Journal-Constitution, the, Sunday, June 12, 1994, "Apparition followers see warning in recent events," by Gayle White

Ball, Ann, *A Litany of Mary*, (Huntington, IN: Our Sunday Visitor Publishing Division, Our Sunday Visitor, Inc., ©1988)

"Betania: Land of Grace," a video narrated by Ricardo Montalban. Directed, written and produced by Drew J. Mariani, Marian Communications, Ltd., ©1993

Billings, Malcolm, *The Cross and the Crescent*, (NY: Sterling Publishing Co., Inc., ©1987)

Blue Army Cell Manual, ©AMI Press, Blue Army of Our Lady of Fátima, Washington, New Jersey, 07882

Brown, Michael H., *The Final Hour*, (Milford, OH: Faith Publishing Company, ©1992)

Brown, Michael H., *The Final Hour: An Urgent Message*, a speech recorded and distributed by The Mary Foundation

Cambridge Medieval History, the Volume VI: Victory of the Papacy, (Cambridge University Press, ©1964)

Campolo, Tony, "Take the Challenge! The Kingdom of Ticky-Tack: Being A Live Christian in a Dead World," Produced and directed by Peter Larson. A Zondervan Video Release, ©1992. All rights reserved

Caritas of Birmingham, quarterly newsletters, ©1991-94, Caritas of Birmingham, Our Lady Queen of Peace Drive, Sterrett, AL 35147

Catechism of the Catholic Church, the (Washington, DC: United States Catholic Conference, Inc., ©1994)

Colson, Charles, with Vaughn, Ellen Santilli, *Kingdoms in Conflict*, (A copublication of William Morrow and Zondervan Publishing House, ©1987)

Cranston, Ruth, *The Miracle of Lourdes*, (New York: Doubleday & Company, Inc., ©1955, 1983, 1988)

Cruz, Joan Carroll, *Eucharistic Miracles and Eucharistic Phenomena in the Lives of the Saints*, (Rockford, IL: TAN Books and Publishers, Inc., ©1987)

Daniel-Rops, Henri, *This is the Mass*, as celebrated by Archbishop Fulton J. Sheen, (New York: Hawthorn Books, Inc., ©1958)

de Montfort, Louis, *The Secret of the Rosary*, (NY: Montfort Publications, ©1965-92) trans. Mary Barbour, T.O.P.

Documents of the Christian Church, Bettenson, Henry S., (London: Oxford University Press, ©1963)

Dreams, Visions & Prophecies of Don Bosco, Brown, Eugene M., ed., (New Rochelle, NY: Don Bosco Publications, ©1986)

Duggan, Paul E., *The Assumption Dogma: Some Reactions and Ecumenical Implications in the Thought of English-Speaking Theologians*, (Dayton, OH: International Marian Research Institute, ©1989)

Encyclopedic Dictionary of Religion, volume A-E, (Washington, DC: Corpus Publications, ©1979)

Evangelicals and Catholics Working Together: The Christian Mission in the Third Millennium, March 29, 1994

Eyewitness to History, John Carey, ed., (Cambridge, MA: Harvard University Press, ©1987)

Fathers of the Church, the, Schopp, Ludwig, ed., (Washington, DC: The Catholic University of America Press, ©1947)

First Mass Book, (New York: Catholic Book Publishing Co., ©1970-88)

Flick, Alexander Clarence, Ph.D., Litt.D., *The Rise of the Mediaeval Church*, (New York: The Knickerbocker Press, ©1909)

Flynn, Ted and Maureen, *The Thunder of Justice*, (Sterling, VA: MaxKol Communications, Inc., ©1993)

Fox, John, *Fox's Book of Martyrs*, (Grand Rapids, MI: Zondervan Publishing House, ©1926,1954,1967), Forbush, William Byron, D.D., ed.

Gentry, Dr. Kenneth L. Jr., *Before Jerusalem Fell: Dating the Book of Revelation*, (Tyler, TX: Institute for Christian Economics, ©1989)

Glasgow, James, D.D., *The Apocalypse: Translated and Expounded*, (Edinburgh: T. & T. Clark, ©1872)

Graham, Anna, *Diary of a Pilgrim to Medjugorje*, December 4, 1988

Grant, Michael, *The Twelve Caesars*, (New York: Charles Scribner's Sons, © 1975)

Great Encyclical Letters of Pope Leo XIII, the (New York, Cincinnati, Chicago: Benziger Brothers, Printers to the Holy Apostolic See, ©1903)

Haffert, John M., *Russia Will Be Converted*, (Washington, NJ: AMI International Press, ©1950)

Hahn, Scott and Kimberly, *Rome Sweet Home: Our Journey to Catholicism*, (San Francisco, CA: Ignatius Press, ©1993)

Hancock, Ann Marie, *Be A Light: Miracles at Medjugorje*, (Norfolk/Virginia Beach, Virginia: The Donning Company Publishers, ©1988)

Hardon, John A., S. J., *The Modern Catholic Dictionary*, (New York: Doubleday & Company, Inc., ©1966)

Hasler, August Bernhard, *How the Pope Became Infallible: Pius IX and the Politics of Persuasion*, (New York: Doubleday & Company, Inc., ©1981)

Holy Love: Messages from Our Blessed Mother Leading Souls to Holiness, containing the messages of the apparition of Mary to Maureen Hinko, (Seven Hills, OH: Our Lady's Foundation, ©1994)

Kelly, J.N.D., *The Oxford Dictionary of Popes*, (NY: Oxford University Press, ©1986)

Kuntz, J. Gary, *Our Holy Mother of Virtues: Messages for the Harvest*, Volume 1, (Denver, CO: Colorado MIR Center, ©1992)

Lalonde, Peter, "The Mark of the Beast," produced by Peter Lalonde and Tim Deibler, An Omega-Letter Video Production, ©1992. All rights reserved

Lindsey, Hal with Carlson, C. C., *The Late Great Planet Earth*, (Grand Rapids, MI: Zondervan Publishing House, ©1970)

Llorente, Juan Antonio, *A Critical History of the Inquisition of Spain*, (Williamstown, MA: The John Lilburne Company, Publishers, ©1967. First English translation, 1823)

Lord, Bob & Penny, *The Many Faces of Mary: A Love Story*, (Westlake Village, CA: Journeys of Faith, ©1987)

Lord, Bob & Penny, *This is My Body, This is My Blood: Book II*, (Westlake Village, CA: Journeys of Faith, ©1994)

Lord, Bob and Penny, *This is My Body, This is My Blood: Book I*, (Westlake Village, CA: Journeys of Faith, ©1986)

Macfarlane, Sr., Bud, M.I., of the Mary Foundation, from his speech entitled "Marian Apparitions Explained," recorded on May 18, 1991 at St. Leo's Catholic Church, Elmwood, NJ

Macfarlane, Sr., Bud, M.I., of the Mary Foundation, from the tape, "Update on Marian Apparitions," recorded on March 25, 1992 at Sacred Heart Catholic Church, Wadsworth, OH

Macfarlane, Sr., Bud, M.I., of the Mary Foundation, from his speech entitled, "The Coming Tribulations," recorded on August, 7, 1993,

Westlake, Ohio, delivered to a group of Mary Foundation friends and benefactors

"Marian Apparitions of the 20th Century: A Message of Urgency," a video narrated by Ricardo Montalban. Produced and written by Drew J. Mariani and Anne McGeehan-McGlone. Directed by Drew J. Mariani. Produced at the Eternal Word Television Network, Birmingham, AL. Marian Communications, Ltd., ©1991, International Copyrights Reserved

Marnham, Patrick, *Lourdes: A Modern Pilgrimage*, (New York: Coward, McCann & Geoghegan, Inc., ©1980)

Mary of Agreda, *Mystical City of God*, Volume IV, *The Coronation*, (Hammond, IN: W. B. Conkey Company, ©1914)

McBrien, Richard P., *Catholicism*, volume 2, (MN: Winston Press, ©1980)

"Medjugorje: The Lasting Sign," a video narrated by Martin Sheen. Directed by Rob Wallace. Produced by Cinematic Visions, Inc., ©1989, All Rights Reserved

Message network of "Our Lady's Message To The World Through Gianna Talone Sullivan" at St. Joseph's Church, Emmitsburg, MD. Sullivan's messages are from a relatively new apparition and are not yet in publication.

Mir Response, the, published by the MIR Group, New Orleans, LA, 70151, Mimi Kelly, ed.

Miravalle, Mark I., S.T.D., *Mary: Coredemptrix, Mediatrix, Advocate*, (Santa Barbara, CA: Queenship Publishing, ©1993)

Neuner, Josef, S. J. & Roos, Heinrich, S.F., *The Teaching of the Catholic Church*, (New York: The Mercier Press, ©1967)

Newsweek, Vol. 110, July 20, 1987, pg. 55, Woodward, Kenneth L. with Nagorski, Andrew, "Visitations of the Virgin"

O'Carroll, Michael, CSSp, *Medjugorje: Facts, Documents, Theology*, (Dublin, Ireland: Veritas Publications, ©1989)

Oldenbourg, Zoé, *The Crusades*, (NY: Random House, ©1966)

Our Lady Queen of Peace, Special Edition I, 2nd Printing, Winter 1992, Dr. Thomas Petrisko, ed. Pittsburgh Center for Peace, McKees Rocks, PA, 15136

Our Lady's Angels, the official newsletter of the Conversion of Russia Prayer Group, St. Thomas More Center, Denver, Colorado

Peters, Edward, *Inquisition*, (New York: The Free Press, a division of Macmillan, Inc., ©1988)

Pope Boniface VIII, Bull *Unam Sanctam*, from the revision of the text in "*Revue des Questions Historiques,*" July, 1889

Pope Innocent IV, Bull *Ad Extirpanda de Medio Populi Christiani Pravitatis Zizania*, May 15, 1252

Pope John Paul II, Instruction *Inæstimabile Donum,* Sacred Congregation for the Sacraments and Divine Worship: "On Certain

Norms Concerning Worship of the Eucharistic Mystery, " February 24, 1980

Pope John Paul II, June 1993, Seville, Spain. Address to the 45th Eucharistic Congress as recorded in *Signs of the Times*, Volume 6, Number 2, April/May/June 1994 edition, "Perpetual Adoration of the Holy Eucharist," pp.10-11

Pope John Paul II, *Redemptoris Mater,* Sixth Encyclical Letter, March 25, 1987

Pope Leo XIII, Encyclical Letter *Miræ Caritatis*, May 28, 1902

Pope Paul VI, Encyclical Letter *Mysterium Fidei*, September 3, 1965

Pope Pius IX, Papal Bull *Ineffabilis Deus*, 1854

Pope Pius XII, Apostolic Constitution *Munificentissimus Deus*, AAS 42(1950):762

Portalié, Eugène, S.J., *A Guide to the Thought of Saint Augustine*, (Chicago: Henry Regnery Company, ©1960)

Prayer Card, *Remembrance of First Holy Communion*, no. 0065. This card accompanied the New *First Mass Book*, (New York: Catholic Book Publishing Co., ©1970-88)

Reicke, Bo, *The New Testament Era: The World of the Bible from 500 B.C. to A.D. 100*, trans. by David E. Green, (Philadelphia, PA: Fortress, © 1968)

Roth, Cecil, M.A., Ph.D., Oxon., *The Spanish Inquisition*, (New York: W.W. Norton & Company, Inc., ©1964)

Saturday Evening Post, The, February 1980, volume 252, number 1, "The Pilgrim Pope: A Builder of Bridges," by Billy Graham

Select Historical Documents of the Middle Ages, translated and edited by Henderson, Ernest F., A.B., A.M., Ph.D., (London: George Bell and Sons, ©1892)

Signs of the Times, published by Signs of the Times, 109 Executive Drive, Suite D, Sterling, Virginia, 20166, Maureen Flynn, ed.

Sunday Missal Prayerbook and Hymnal for 1994, (NY: Catholic Book Publishing Company, ©1993)

Teachings of the Second Vatican Council, The, (Westminster, MD: The Newman Press, ©1966)

Tennesseean, the, Volume 89, no. 66, March 7, 1993, Associated Press, "Filipinos flock to glimpse vision of Mary," pg. 2A

Time Magazine, Volume 144, Number 26, December 26, 1994/January 2, 1995, "Empire of the Spirit," pp. 53-57

To Bear Witness that I Am the Living Son of God, Vol. 1: Reported Teachings and Messages to the World from Our Lord and Our Loving Mother, (Newington, VA: Our Loving Mother's Children, ©1991)

Turberville, Arthur Stanley, *The Spanish Inquisition*, (Oxford University Press: Archon Books, ©1932)

US News & World Report, October 8, 1979, volume 87, number 15, "America Meets John Paul"

Van Kampen, Robert, *The Sign*, (Wheaton, IL: Crossway Books, ©1992)

Virgin Wholly Marvelous: Praises of Our Lady from the Popes, Councils, Saints, and Doctors of the Church, Peter Brookby, ed., (Cambridge, England: The Ravengate Press, ©1981)

Walsh, William Thomas, *Our Lady of Fátima*, (New York: Doubleday & Company, Inc., ©1947, 1954)

Wanderer, the, "Sacramento Bishop Offers Some Liturgical Reminders," Volume 127, number 32, August 11, 1994. *The Wanderer*, 201 Ohio Street, St. Paul, MN 55107

Washington Post, the, Volume 117, number 313, "For Thousands, the Virgin Mary Is a Vision of Hope," pp. A1,24

Weible, Wayne, *Miracle at Medjugorje: A series of columns on a modern-day supernatural religious event,* "You are my son…" from an article published December 18, 1985

What is Caritas of Birmingham?, a tract explaining the mission of *Caritas of Birmingham*

Words From Heaven: Messages of Our Lady from Medjugorje, 5th ed., (Birmingham, AL: Saint James Publishing Company, ©1991). The authors wished to be known only as, "Two friends of Medjugorje."

Zimdars-Swartz, Sandra L., *Encountering Mary*, (New York: Princeton University Press, ©1991)

Zins, Robert M., Th.M., *Romanism: The Relentless Roman Catholic Assault on the Gospel of Jesus Christ,* (Huntsville, AL: White Horse Publications, ©1995)

Glossary

Adoration of the Wafer (see Eucharistic Adoration)

Altar: The 'table' at the front of a Catholic Church. The altar is where the Sacrifice of the Mass is offered in reparation for the sin of the world.

Apparition: A visual supernatural encounter.

Assumption: The doctrine that was proclaimed by Pope Pius XII in 1950, declaring that Mary had been taken up, body and soul, into Heaven upon the completion of her earthly ministry.

***Ave Maria*:** Latin for the prayer 'Hail Mary.'

Benediction: A ritual during which a consecrated wafer is placed upon the altar for adoration and meditation.

Bishop: A member of the Church hierarchy. Above a priest, but below an archbishop or a cardinal.

Brown Scapular (see Scapular, Brown)

Bull, Papal: As in "bulletin." An official document issued by the pope.

Cardinal: A member of the Catholic Church hierarchy. Above an archbishop but below the pope.

Caritas: A Latin wording meaning 'Love.'

***Caritas of Birmingham*:** An organization dedicated exclusively to the worldwide distribution of the messages from the apparition of Mary at Medjugorje, Bosnia.

Centenary: A celebration honoring the 100-year anniversary of an important event.

Chalice: An ornate cup or goblet in which wine is poured before it is consecrated by a priest during the Sacrifice of the Mass.

Communion: The memorial meal which was instituted by Jesus Christ. Christians celebrate communion to honor Christ by partaking of bread and wine in memory of His death on the cross. In Catholicism, the bread and wine are believed to be the True Presence of Christ--that is, the bread really is His flesh, and the wine really is His blood.

Confession, Sacrament of: One of the sacraments instituted by the Catholic Church, whereby a sinner confesses sins and obtains absolution, or cleansing of those sins, from God, through the mediation of a priest.

Consecrated: A term describing the wine and host, or bread, that have been through the process of transubstantiation by a priest, and are therefore considered to be the True Physical Presence of Jesus Christ in the form of real flesh and real blood. Also in reference to devotion to Mary, as in 'Consecrated to the Immaculate Heart.'

Co-redemptress (see also Redemptress): A title given to Mary with the understanding that she works in cooperation with Christ to bear the burden of the sin of the world.

Coronation (of Mary) (see also Mysteries, and Rosary): The last of the five Glorious Mysteries of the Rosary. It refers to the belief that Mary, upon her ascension into Heaven, was crowned Queen of Heaven and Earth.

Corruption: Bodily decay in the grave. This is in reference to the belief that Mary's body did not undergo corruption in the tomb. This belief was necessitated by the Immaculate Conception dogma, and was used as a premise for the Assumption dogma.

Dance of the Sun (see Miracle of the Sun)

Diocese (see also Parish): A term used to define a geographic boundary within the Catholic Church. A diocese is to an archdiocese as a county is to a state.

Ecstasy: A term used to describe the state of extreme happiness and satisfaction that visionaries experience during an apparition, inner locution, or other form of paranormal interaction with the apparition of Mary.

Eucharist (see also Communion): From the Greek, *eucharisteo*, or "give thanks." The term is used for the Catholic Eucharist, or thank offering of bread and wine.

Eucharistic Adoration: Time spent on one's knees in front of a consecrated host, or wafer, in reverence and adoration as if it were truly Jesus Christ, Himself.

***ex cathedra*:** Literally, "From the Chair." That is, the Chair of St. Peter. When a pope speaks with respect to the definition of an article of Christian faith and morals, he speaks *ex cathedra*. It is held among Catholics that when the pope speaks *ex cathedra*, he cannot err.

Exposition: A term describing the placing of the Eucharist on display, or exposing it, for adoration.

Feast Day: A special day during the Church calendar year set aside for prayer about, and meditation on, a Church-centered event in history. For example, the Feast of the Assumption is celebrated on August 15 of every year.

***fides catholica*:** Obligatory faith. A matter of doctrine which those who deny cannot legitimately be called Catholics. The Assumption dogma, for example, is a matter of *fides catholica,* or obligatory faith.

***fides humana*:** Non-obligatory faith, or human faith. A matter of doctrine which is acceptable to the Catholic Church, but is not required of Catholics. Belief in the apparitions of Mary is a matter of *fides humana.*

Genuflect, genuflection: The act of showing reverence to the Eucharist by bowing or kneeling in the presence of it. This is also done when coming into the presence of the pope, a cardinal or other high-ranking clergyman. A proper genuflection usually involves a deep bow on one or both knees, and making the sign of the cross. For the clergyman, the genuflection represents honor and respect, but for the Eucharist, it is an act of worship.

Holy Father: Another name for the pope.

Host: Another term for a Communion wafer, or Eucharistic wafer. It comes from the Latin *hostia*, meaning 'sacrificial victim,' or 'victim of sacrifice.'

Immaculate Conception: The doctrine that was proclaimed by Pope Pius IX in 1854, declaring that Mary had been conceived without sin, that is, immaculately, and was therefore born outside of the bloodline of Adam.

Immaculate Heart of Mary: Usually pictured as a heart pierced by a sword, in reference to Simeon's prophecy in Luke 2:35.

Ineffabilis Deus: The Papal Bull (1854) in which Pope Pius IX declared that the Immaculate Conception was a divinely revealed doctrine of the Catholic faith.

Infallibility (see also, *ex cathedra*): The belief that the pope, when speaking *ex cathedra*, cannot err.

Locution, or Inner Locution: A paranormal experience during which the recipient hears a supernatural voice, but not through the physical ear.

Mass (see Sacrifice of the Mass)

Mediatrix: A title given to Mary with the understanding that she mediates between God and man, or between Jesus and man.

Miracle of the Sun: A phenomenon that accompanies many Marian apparitions. Eyewitnesses claim that they see the sun spinning, changing to all colors of the rainbow, and then plummeting to earth and rising again. Less dramatic accounts at various apparition sites still describe the changing colors and the distinct appearance that the sun is getting closer, then farther away.

Miraculous Medal: A medal given to Saint Catherine Labouré by an apparition of Mary in 1830. On the front, it is stamped with an image of Mary with the words, "O, Mary, conceived without sin, pray for us who have recourse to thee." On the back is an image of the Immaculate Heart of Mary alongside the Sacred Heart of Jesus, surrounded by twelve stars.

Miter: A crown, or hat, representing the exalted position of a clergyman, e.g., the pope or another bishop.

Monstrance: The display case in which the consecrated host is placed on display, or is exposed, for adoration. The Monstrance is usually in the shape of a sunburst, but a cross-shaped Monstrance can be seen on the front and back covers of this book.

Munificentissimus Deus: The Apostolic Constitution (1950) in which Pope Pius XII declared that the Assumption of Mary was a divinely revealed doctrine of the Catholic faith.

Mysteries, Glorious (5) (see also Rosary): Each of the Glorious Mysteries represents a meditation on an event for one decade of the Rosary, that is, for ten Hail Marys. The five Glorious Mysteries are: The Resurrection, the Ascension of Jesus, the Descent of the Holy Spirit, the Assumption of Mary, and the Coronation of Mary as Queen of Heaven and Earth.

Mysteries , Joyful (5) (see also Rosary): Each of the Joyful Mysteries represents a meditation on an event for one decade of the Rosary, that is, for ten Hail Marys. The five Joyful Mysteries are: The Annunciation to Mary, the Visitation of Mary, the Nativity, the Presentation in the Temple, and the Finding of Jesus in the Temple.

Mysteries, Sorrowful (5) (see also Rosary): Each of the Sorrowful Mysteries represents a meditation on an event for one decade of the Rosary, that is, for ten Hail Marys. The five Sorrowful Mysteries are: The Agony in the Garden, the Scourging at the Pillar, the Crowning with Thorns, the Carrying of the Cross, and the Crucifixion.

Neck (of the Body of Christ): A name referring to Mary. It stems from the belief that she is above the Body proper, but below Christ, the Head, and actually joins the two.

Obligatory Faith (see *fides catholica*)

Ordinary: A bishop with special jurisdiction over a diocese. The ordinary oversees all of the bishops of a diocese.

Our Holy Father: Another name for the pope.

Papal Bull (see Bull, Papal)

Parish (see also Diocese): A Catholic congregation. A parish is to a diocese as a city is to a county.

Phenomenon of the Sun (see Miracle of the Sun)

Pilgrim: Someone who journeys to the site of an apparition or Eucharistic miracle

Pilgrimage: A pious endeavor to visit a shrine or site of an apparition.

Purgatory: A Catholic belief in a place between Heaven and hell where sinners, through punishments, pay off the balance of the price for their sin before entering into Heaven. It is held that souls in purgatory can obtain earlier entrance into Heaven if they, while living, were devoted to Mary through the Rosary and the Brown Scapular, or through the Sacrifice of the Mass, or both.

Pyx: A small round container used to transport a consecrated wafer, or host.

Redemptress (see also Co-redemptress): A title given to Mary with the understanding that she suffers in order to redeem sinful man by paying a portion of the price for sin.

Roman Pontiff: Another name for the pope.

Rosary (see also Mysteries): A method of prayer. The Rosary contains 54 beads connected in a loop which begins and ends with five beads and a crucifix. Each bead represents a "Hail Mary" or an "Our Father." It is recited by praying one "Our Father," 10 "Hail Marys," and one "Glory Be" which makes one decade. A complete Rosary is prayed by reciting 15 "Our Fathers," 150 "Hail Marys," and 15 "Glory Be's."

Sacred Heart of Jesus: Usually pictured as a heart surrounded by thorns to represent the suffering of Christ on the cross.

Sacrifice of the Mass: The religious ritual during which bread and wine, having been changed into the body and blood of Christ, are offered as a sacrifice in reparation for the sin of the world.

Scapular, Brown : Two brown pieces of cloth held together by strings and worn over the shoulders so that the cloth pieces rest simultaneously on the chest and back of the wearer. The Brown Scapular was given to St. Simon Stock in 1251 by an apparition of Mary, with the promise that anyone who wore it would not go to hell.

Sign of the Cross: Much like an 'amen,' the sign of the cross ends a prayer, or is used in blessing someone. It is done with the hand by tracing the four points of the cross either over one's own torso (forehead to chest, then shoulder to shoulder), or in front of the person being 'crossed.'

Species: A term used to refer to either or both of the elements of Communion. For example, the bread is one specie, the wine is another, and together they represent both species.

Tabernacle: A place where something sacred is stored, usually in reference to the consecrated bread and wine.

Transubstantiation: The process by which bread and wine become the real body and blood of Jesus Christ during the Sacrifice of the Mass. Only a Catholic priest can perform transubstantiation.

Visionaries: Those who actually see apparitions or experience inner locutions, and receive messages.

Wafer (see Host, Eucharist)

Subject Index

Names of visionaries and locutionists in **bold face**.

Scripture Index

Tim Kauffman was born in 1965 in San Diego, California, and raised in a military family. He spent his childhood traveling through and living in the states of Hawaii, California, Massachusetts, Oregon and Colorado, respectively. He received his Bachelor of Science in Mechanical Engineering from the University of Colorado at Boulder in 1989, and is now employed as an engineer with the National Aeronautics and Space Administration in Huntsville, Alabama.

Additional Titles Available From

Geese in their Hoods: Selected Writings on Roman Catholicism by Charles Haddon Spurgeon
compiled & edited by Timothy F. Kauffman, 204 p.... $9.95

A collection of Spurgeon's writings on a topic of great importance today. Spurgeon's greatest criticism wasn't of Rome, but of *Protestants* who wandered after her. Over 30 of Spurgeon's finest essays and tracts, accompanied by the original woodcarvings.

Romanism: The Relentless Roman Catholic Assault on the Gospel of Jesus Christ!
by Robert M. Zins, Th.M., 280 p. $8.95

Rob Zins' cuts to the heart of the matter in *Romanism*, and asks the question, "What is the only ground of our justification?" Rome's answer is different from the Bible's. Zins looks beyond the surface differences between the Church of Rome and Biblical Christianity, and strikes at the very heart of the Romanist system: the different gospel of indefinite and incremental justification by works. Zins' work is an excellent resource for anyone who desires a deeper understanding of the difference between Romanism and Christianity.

Graven Bread: The Papacy, the Apparitions of Mary, and the Worship of the Bread of the Altar
by Timothy F. Kauffman, 206 p. $7.95

In *Graven Bread* Kauffman explores the implications of the Roman belief that the communion bread contains not only the body and blood, but the *soul and divinity* of Christ Himself. The logical conclusion, and what Rome actually teaches, is that the bread should be worshipped—this is nothing short of idolatry.

Quite Contrary: A Biblical Reconsideration of the Apparitions of Mary
by Timothy F. Kauffman, 206 p. $7.95

Perhaps you have heard of the many appearances of Mary in the world. That something is appearing as Mary is well documented. But what are these "Marys" teaching? Their many statements betray their origins, as Kauffman examines their words in light of the Bible to show that these apparitions are not whom they claim to be.

Formidable Truth: A Vindication of Loraine Boettner
by Robert M. Zins, Th.M., 54 p. $4.95

No Protestant scholar has come under more fire from Rome this century than Loraine Boettner, author of the exposé of Roman dogma and doctrine, *Roman Catholicism*. Zins comes to Boettner's defense to show that in spite of the many unfounded accusations of poor scholarship, Boettner still stands. *Formidable Truth* originally appeared as Appendix II in Zins' *Romanism* under the title, *Veritas Formidabilis*.

On the Edge of Apostasy: The Evangelical Romance with Rome, by Robert M. Zins, Th.M., 280 p.....................$10.95

Just as Paul once asked, "...what fellowship hath righteousness with unrighteousness? and what communion hath light with darkness?" (2 Corinthians 6:14), Zins asks, "What fellowship hath Protestants with Romanists?" Knowing that Protestants and Roman Catholics adhere to two different gospels, Zins concludes that many of today's evangelicals who are increasingly complicitous with Rome are wandering dangerously close to the edge of apostasy.

(There is an additional fee to cover the expenses of shipping and handling: $3.00 per book, plus 0.50 for each additional item to the same address. See order form, facing page, for details.)

To contact White Horse Publications, please write to:

White Horse Publications
PO Box 2398
Huntsville, AL 35804-2398

or call toll free:

1-800-867-2398

White Horse Publications
http://whpub.com

Order Form

(photocopy this form and mail it with a check made payable to White Horse Publications, PO Box 2398, Huntsville, AL 35804-2398, USA)

Name ____

Address ____

____

City ____________________ State ______ Zip __________

Geese in their Hoods: Selected Writings on Roman Catholicism by Charles Haddon Spurgeon
compiled & edited by Timothy F. Kauffman, 204 p.
....$9.95 x ____qty. = ______

Romanism: The Relentless Roman Catholic Assault on the Gospel of Jesus Christ!
by Robert M. Zins, Th.M., 280 p.
....$8.95 x ____qty. = ______

Graven Bread: The Papacy, the Apparitions of Mary, and the Worship of the Bread of the Altar
by Timothy F. Kauffman, 206 p.
....$7.95 x ____qty. = ______

Quite Contrary: A Biblical Reconsideration of the Apparitions of Mary
by Timothy F. Kauffman, 206 p.
....$7.95 x ____qty. = ______

Formidable Truth: A Vindication of Loraine Boettner
by Robert M. Zins, Th.M., 54 p.
....$4.95 x ____qty. = ______

On the Edge of Apostasy: The Evangelical Romance with Rome,
by Robert M. Zins, Th.M., 280 p.
....$10.95 x ____qty. = ______

shipping ($3.00 for one item,
plus .50 for each additional
item to the same address) .... $________

Total .... $________

(International orders: checks must be drawn on a US Bank. *Add $5 for shipping)*